The year 2009 marks the 100th anniversary of Filippo Tommaso Marinetti's *Futurist Manifesto.* On February 20, 1909, the *Manifesto* of the controversial Italian poet was published on the front page of *Le Figaro* in Paris and is considered by many to have laid the fertile ground for the ensuing Dada movement. This is the perfect occasion to revive a piece of history that has shaped the art world of the 20th century, as it continues to exercise a vital influence on contemporary visual and literary art.

This book is also a daring attempt by the author to update the notion of Dada to the 21st century and to introduce what he has come to define as *the Dada-Gene,* a common denominator shared by all humans that enhances creativity and resourcefulness.

Faustino Quintanilla,
Director, the QCC Gallery/Museum
Queens, New York

Rudy Ernst

THE STORY OF DADA

...and How to Activate Your Dada-Gene

Library of Congress Cataloging-in-Publication Data

Ernst, Rudy, 1937-
The Story of Dada
And How to Activate Your Dada-Gene – 1st ed.
Nov. 17, 2009

Published by QCC Art Gallery Press,
The City University of New York, Bayside, N.Y.
© 2009 by Rudy Ernst

ISBN: 0976475685
EAN-13: 9780976475682
LCCN: 2009048990
N6537.E76A35 2009
709.04'062—dc22

QCC Art Gallery
The City University of New York

Front Cover:
Rudy Ernst - from his "Ready Made, Reverse Engineered Sculptures:"
Moonshine Sonata – 26" high, 2009
Antique Tin Plate, Aluminum Gearing, Metallic Burners
Photography by Arpi Pap

Back Cover:
Rudy Ernst: Dada Action Painting at the QCC Gallery – May 2008
Photography by Arpi Pap
Cover design and execution by Rudy Ernst © 2009

The Author

Rudy Ernst's life was marked by extremes. After his Ph.D. in economics in Lausanne, Switzerland, he suffered a near-death experience with a 32-minute cardiac arrest, following a horrific accident. In 1982, he pulled the plug from corporate life and immigrated to Manhattan with his wife and two sons, to become a painter, sculptor, writer, philosopher and a poet. Obsessed with the act of creation, he then lived years in isolation in his Manhattan studio.

Ernst shares his time between the metropolis of Manhattan and the rural life of the Blue Ridge Mountains in southwest Virginia, where he built a large studio back in 1988. He is also solidly anchored both in the analog and in the digital worlds, and his *Reverse Engineered Readymade Sculptures* distinctly carry his signature.

In 2007, Ernst became a self-declared Dadaist, and in 2008 he did his first Dada action paintings in large New York gallery spaces.

Ernst is fluent in German, French, English, Spanish and Italian and has an intimate knowledge of these cultures.

PART I:
DADA IN CONTEXT

Chapter 1

Describing the Dada-Gene

About this Book

In September of 2008, I decided to write this book about the Dada-Gene. While filling page after page, I was happy to see how easily the chapters were flowing into my pen. If it continued like that, my manuscript would be finished in just a few weeks, ready for publication.

So I thought. But that was before I started my in-depth research on the many different aspects of the Dada topic: Who were the precursors of the different Dada movements? How did they interrelate? In what countries were they active? How did the movements fall apart? And why did the word "Dada" inspire the imagination of so many generations to come?

I always knew that the humanities are not an exact science, and that the arts probably stand out as its most difficult field to be accurately understood and categorized in a comprehensive book. But writing about Dada took the notion of complexity to an unexpectedly higher level.

In 1916, the "Dada" name is officially introduced by the Zurich Group of the Cabaret Voltaire. From there, it spreads into many countries around the globe, becomes influenced by the psychoanalysts Sigmund Freud (1856-1936) and Carl Jung (1875-1961), falls apart, and in 1922 becomes absorbed by the Surrealist movement in Paris. In the late 1950s, the abstract impressionist painters of the "New York School" revive the term under the newly introduced idea of "Neo-Dadaism," but the word doesn't pass the test of time. In subsequent years, however, the Dada idea is resurrected by many follow-up endeavors trying to jump on the Dada bandwagon, right up to the present time.

*

I wrote a number of essays about the many Dada players and the movements that were influenced by the Dada idea, and, after months of struggles, ended up with papers full of different angles and individual approaches to the subject matter, which I then tried to interweave. To no avail: Instead of getting a grip on the topic, the outcome remained not only incomplete as a reference book on Dada, but had become confused and was falling apart. What's even worse, my idea of introducing the "Dada-Gene" had become lost among an overflow of irrelevant information.

The way back to my original subject was painful: I had to eliminate the overwhelming part of my manuscript and start afresh, thus confirming the theory that a book must be written seven times over before going to press.

Finally, I may expose myself to the criticism of being not enough streamlined, of having too broad of an approach to the Dada subject. I have extensively thought about this, but finally chose to branch out into a number of global aspects, because the Dada movement did not happen out of context. Therefore, a more limited approach to the Dada subject would have cut out too many important aspects of the topic that I wanted to embrace.

What is Dada?

"What is Dada? You have become a Dadaist? Have you lost it?" Such were the questions I was getting all day long from those of my friends who are not familiar with art history.

"Yes," I replied. "I may have lost it. Indeed. But then, has the whole world not lost it altogether? Are the universal insanities of wars, lies, deceptions, misleading marketing schemes, and an out-of-whack financial system not even more insane than a child-like approach that goes back to the sound of words rather than to their corrupted meanings?"

I have chosen a good-natured approach to those heated discussions about politics, religion and the economy. My answer is that the best way to preserve friendships is to interject periodically my ready-made contribution: "The answer is always Dada!"

How I became a Dadaist

When my friends ask me when and why I became a Dadaist, I say: "Since 2007, when I first realized the full extent of the world's *Dada Economy*, and how unstable the global socio-politico-economical system has become."

I believe that the times we live in are evocative of those days in 1916, when the European Dada movement first came to life. Unfortunately, history repeats itself, though it always comes to us in a new dress that is not easily recognizable by a young generation.

Dada was based on the fundamental idea of "form over substance" in an environment where the word "substance" had become meaningless. Today, we lament the progressive impoverishment of the middle classes and revolt against the excesses of capitalism as Karl Marx saw it. And, once again, we fight this dreadful development with shallow and empty words in an environment where the word "substance" has become meaningless.

Dada in Cyber Space

Let's take a moment to google the word "Dada" on the Internet. As I write this paragraph, in early 2009, the result totals 20 pages of no less than 56,800,000 hits ranging from music to arts, to shoes, poetry and many more!

It would be way beyond the scope of this book to go into the detail of those manifold Dada-related subjects. But have a look for yourself. Doesn't that tell us something about the popularity of the word *Dada*?

Why Dada?

Still, one might wonder why I chose the word "Dada," which is so heavily loaded with much written-about historic burdens, rather than creating a new word.

My reasons are that the word Dada itself evokes fascination, and that it is precisely the rich history of the various Dada movements that I would like to build upon.

Imagine an object standing on a theatre stage and bathed in the limelight of a single light beam. Now add an additional light source onto that object, but from a different angle. Suddenly, many previously unseen details of that identical object become visible and put its entire appearance into a new light. This is the effect I would like to achieve with the subject of Dada.

One aspect of this book is to inform how Dada has influenced the global art scene during the 20th century and how every major artist of that period was in one way or another involved in the Dada or the ensuing Surrealist movements. I want to show how the word "Dada" stubbornly stayed alive through many cycles and art movements of recent history.

But this book contains more than a historic rundown of facts. It reveals my personal thought process and suggests that we all carry within ourselves a creative cord, which I have come to describe as "The Dada-Gene."

Explaining The Dada-Gene

Among the most basic principles of life are the notions of "ego" and "instinct of self-preservation." They appear to be the driving forces in organisms as small as the E-coli bacteria.

While pondering upon the subject, I came to realize that the notion of ego probably also is the common denominator underlying the human drive towards resourcefulness. That urge to take matters into one's own hands, to stay alive and protect the family rather than following orders and depending on any other authority. That's when it dawned on me that we all share a more or less explicit concern and desire to activate our resourcefulness, longing to prepare for a better future for our next of kin and ourselves.

I came to call it the Dada-Gene.

As I became aware of, and begun reflecting upon, my own Dada-Gene, I concluded by extension that each of us must carry that very same gene. All I had to do was to define it.

The Dada-Gene also appears to be a fabulous weapon of self-preservation. It enables us to detach ourselves from the misery and turmoil of the outside world and to escape into the realm of our inner dream world. It responds to our human yearning for independence and resourcefulness, of which we seem to be more in need today than ever before.

We are who we are. Nobody can change that, nor take it away. But while we each carry almost the identical genes as the rest of humanity, a long trail of personal history individualizes us into having become Joe, or Jane, or Tanaka.

We are born from our mother's womb with all the specific gene features that condition our personal health, our looks and our intellectual features. But we are also born into environments that condition who we are going to be as we grow up. Later, we may study, or not, enlist in the army, work for a bank, or just sit on our doorsteps and remain idle. We may be exposed to the horrors of war, live in a pampered environment, go hungry, or even become murderers. All those lifelong imperatives, choices and experiences contribute to differentiate each one of us from all the other human beings and help generating a uniquely individualized life.

A single prevailing factor in all of humanity is our genetic code, which is made up of billions of bits and pieces that define every particular part of our human cell colony. One of those bits and pieces is the Dada-Gene, our personal ability to express individuality in one form or another, be it artistic or otherwise. The Dada-Gene may be invisible to the naked eye, but it is omnipresent, and it is responsible for each one of us to feel an urge of self-expression.

Since we all grow up in different environments, we tend to pass through a mental filter the meanings of what other people seem to say, so that they fit the views that our own environment has programmed us to understand. In other words: People don't hear what we say, but rather what they understand, which is often radically different, because of the environment in which they were brought up. That environment generates what I call "the uniform of the mind," a uniform every bit as scary as the uniforms worn by soldiers or policemen. Discovering our Dada-Gene is a way to escape from those imperatives that society imposes on us by taking time out and reflecting about who we really are.

My personal focus has primarily been on the artistic expression of the Dada-Gene, and more generally on the expression of beauty and harmony. The Dada-Gene promotes awareness to details of everyday life that we routinely tend to overlook or accept as self-understood. It also acts as a precious defense mechanism that enables us to isolate ourselves from nasty environments and to focus on elements of beauty and harmony that sometimes may be found under the most unexpected circumstances.

The following story of a group of neighbors in the city of Berlin during World War II comes to mind. It was the middle of the night. They had just plundered the lavish wine cellar of a bombed-out villa and were now standing atop the ruins of their houses, from where they witnessed a fierce bombing attack by the Allied Air Forces. Suddenly, amidst that horror scenario, and in a Nero-like fashion, they began indulging in the admiration of the unique spectacle of their burning city, while thoroughly enjoying an exquisite bottle of wine and chanting their old student songs…

Chapter 2
Today's World

1. War of the Minds

In a way, today's environment is not unlike those turbulent times of 1916, when the Dada movement first came to life. The difference is that, in our Western World, we are not exposed to a war fought with guns, but rather what I call a "war of the minds."

Each one of our lives is overshadowed by a myriad of near-abstract numbers reaching into the hundreds of trillions of dollars of what is commonly referred to as "Derivatives," as well as mountains of government debts, which nobody - not even the experts - really understand or can put into perspective.

Due to the Internet, our planet has shrunk dramatically and is now globally in a state of confusion and disorder, the likes of which we haven't seen in recorded history. Our economic models are collapsing, and real wars are looming in many corners of the world. Conventional reasoning has lead to dead ends wherever we look, and political discussions have become ever more heated and remote from ordinary citizens.

In the old Soviet-Union, the word used to be that if you wanted to understand the truth, you had to read the party newspaper *Pravda* and interpret its reported "facts" by the exact opposite in order to get to the truth. But, after a while, the people became so accustomed to the lies of the press, that the government had to outsmart them again by taking their disinformation tactics to an even higher level of deception: They now reported the facts exactly as they were, hoping the people would look for the truth as being the exact opposite.

Haven't we reached an almost similar state of mind in our "free world" today?

One of the dialectic theories teaches that in a discussion about an affirmation of facts, the exact opposite is equally true. It is the well-known communist antithesis that has been borrowed from a Buddhist assertion of the very same basic idea, but applied in a devious manner.

And since people are never persuaded by what we say, but rather by what they understand (which can be dramatically different), it explains why rational arguments never win any debate. Isn't that living proof that we have come to live in a Dada World?

When we turn on our TV set, the chances of seeing a "breaking news" story is probably fifty percent. It could be a cat that fell into a sewer and was miraculously rescued, or a bloodbath created by a suicide bomber in the Middle East, or a new anti-cholesterol drug. It doesn't matter, for as long as we get a newsflash every fifteen seconds when we stare at our TV set.

What we are witnessing may well be more than just the failure of a few individuals or a group of individuals. What is happening feels more like a systemic collapse of a culture living on borrowed time that has increasingly gone wrong for nearly a century. A system, which has been kept alive artificially by mortgaging the future from one economic quarter to the next and has become a self-understood routine for the past sixty years. A system also where the good citizens of this country have come to be represented by a disconnected bunch of career politicians in Washington, of which a large majority are lawyers and former prosecutors and should be sent home every eight or twelve years to learn how to make a living by running a real business.

Isn't this the perfect time for a suggestion to discover our own creative Dada-Gene, at a time where so many things are going wrong and need to be addressed at so many different levels?

2. The Age of Cyber Space

The Strange Context of Human Evolution

How farfetched is it to remind ourselves that there have been 80,000 generations of human beings before us and that less than one half of one percent of those generations have been living within the past 2,000 years?

*

Amidst a zillion thoughts that cross human minds every day, how much time do we devote to such important reflections? We are so very busy coping with all the pressing problems of our daily lives that the almost incomprehensible, yet so obvious, basic history of our specie appears not to bother our intellect for a single moment.

If I can get you, Dear Reader, to close your eyes for just a moment and reflect upon the simple idea of where we are all coming from in a historical prospective, one of the main purposes of this book has been achieved. That single minute of inward look may open up an entirely new prospective upon your life, and indeed prepare you for activating your own Dada-Gene.

But I have no illusions: We are all so very driven by apparently much more pressing matters, that we may find it difficult, if not impossible, to redirect our priorities away from what we feel to be our next most urgent challenges of the day.

Let us analyze the broader context of the most pressing global challenges that we are facing.

20th Century: Becoming Digital

If we accept that humanity has doubled its global knowledge every ten to fifteen years during the 20th century, then global human knowledge would have exploded 1000-fold since the year 1900!

When I grew up in a small rural village in Switzerland, there were no electronic calculators, nor even electric typewriters. Multiplying and dividing had to be done in handwriting or with a logarithmic slide ruler.

When a man in a remote valley came up with an idea that nobody ever had before on his side of the mountain, he was believed to be a genius. Today, barely sixty years later, that remote valley in the Swiss mountains is open to the vast territory of the Internet, where millions of geniuses share their ideas and build on each other's achievements at a breathtaking pace, while making their revolutionary ideas the standard platform for the next computer generation, just four or five years down the road, and ready to carry on the torch to previously unimagined higher levels.

Since the dawn of time, people were dominated by leaders: In ancient Egypt by pharaohs, during roman times by emperors, in the 20th century by dictators. With the availability of instant communication and information due to television and the Internet, a fundamental change has taken place. We have indeed entered an era of entirely leveled plain fields, where class distinctions have disappeared.

The most flagrant external sign of this evolution is our uniform dress code.

When I grew up, factory workers never dared to wear shirts and ties other than for church on a Sunday morning, nor would an adult member of the "upper class" dream of wearing sloppy blue jeans, as has become the accepted standard today.

When I grew up, looks were everything. Today, you can be unshaved, walk around with holes in your pants - it doesn't matter. In fact, the opposite is almost true: The sloppier you look, the more extravagant (and therefore interesting) you appear to be.

21st Century: The Age of Cyberspace

Already, our young generations are living a double-life: one related to their physical presence, the other in the virtual reality of cyberspace. And that virtual existence has become an addictive drug almost as powerful as any sniffed-up or injected substance. In South Korea, today, there are almost as many mental hospitals dealing with a generation of intoxicated cyberspace addicts as those affected by chemical drugs.

Cyberspace-related connections have replaced the social gatherings of the good old clubs and the get-togethers in our former village squares. Physical closeness has yielded to abstract new friendships and shorthand languages in cyberspace that tickle the nervous system of our younger generations in previously unknown ways. Paradoxically, cyberspace friendships are substituting our basic human need for personal closeness. But make no mistake: Physical contact continues to be essential for our human well being, since it relates to our traditional five senses: sight, hearing, touch, smell and taste. Without their involvement, we humans run the danger of becoming imbalanced weirdoes.

De-Personalization of the Individual

Among these new developments, people are slowly ceasing to be "real" persons and, through the Internet, have come to "de-personalize" and in a way become abstract ideas.

The best illustration is the case of today's celebrities whom we all know from the TV and movie screens. They are our household names, bigger than life, and they incarnate what ordinary people dream of being. They are the idols of modern society.

But have you ever met one of those celebrities in person and gone through the agonizing process of seeing your idol fall apart, as you realized that she or he is either not looking the way you imagined, or has a surprisingly low IQ? Yes: those celebrities are just ordinary people, "talents" as they are called in the TV studios, and usually not very funny. And that doesn't even begin to address their marital, family, or drug problems.

A story comes to mind that exemplifies another aspect of what I call de-personalization of the roll model. In 2008, the New York Metropolitan Museum organized an exhibition of Frank Stella, one of the most celebrated visual artists alive. My friend, Jimmy Andrade of the

Knoedler Gallery, had invited me to the opening reception and introduced me to the famous man, who I found to be very nice, humble and likeable. The three of us were standing at the refreshment bar in the splendid hall of Roman sculptures, together with many of the 1,200 personally invited guests. Frank Stella is physically rather short. Nobody around us seemed to recognize him, even though the artist's name was prominently displayed on many huge overhead banners.

After a while of being overlooked and ignored by the barman in front of us, my friend uncharacteristically raised his voice and pointed his finger at Frank Stella. "Do you know who this man is?" No reaction from the barkeeper. "This is Frank Stella," Jimmy shouted over the loud background noise, "the man who is celebrated tonight by all these people." Still, the barman showed no emotion on his bored face, as he continued to drag his feet for another five minutes before finally serving us. He never got the point, thinking Frank Stella was just another impatient man trying to expedite his turn to get a drink.

Hyper Stimulation

While we live in a society where boredom is one of the prevailing feelings and emotions, the exact opposite is equally true when related to our youngest generation, where over-stimulation has become a fact of life - an incredible overflow of information and stimuli wherever we turn our eyes.

The unintended consequence of over-stimulation is already showing in our classrooms, where children are routinely fed with anti-hype medication to combat a growing trend of Attention Deficit Disorder (ADD).

Over-stimulation of our sensory experience is in no way a compensation for, or an escape from, a deeply rooted sense of boredom, because the remedy for boredom is not another passive intake of stimulation. Rather, the solution is to turn inwards onto our own inner being and change from being a "consumer" to becoming an active person, or what I call a "producer."

And How About the Arts?

Where does the art world stand amidst those quantum leaps of technology? It used to be that the arts would act as precursors for historic events of the future. No more, though, in my opinion. The arts have split into two basic currents: the ones that follow the technical evolution of the computer age and are primarily related to commercial marketing projects, and the traditional "collectible" art that investors and would-like-to-be-collectors hang on their walls or store in warehouses, in the hope of raking in some hefty windfall profits after the artist may have the decency to die...

Other than in the field of photography, or maybe in the case of certain memorabilia, few art collectors are ready to jump into the age of cyberspace. The computer and Internet revolution, along with what has been called a "paperless society," simply took the traditionally conservative art market by surprise.

As for myself, I have tried since the early 1990s to introduce cutting-edge technologies into my own artistic expressions by what I call CAA, my "Computer Aided Art" images. To no avail! Nobody paid attention. And when I had a series of exhibitions, in the early years of the new millennium, my works were patently ignored.

As recently as 2006, the well-known art critic Irving Sandler dedicated his book *From Avant-Garde To Pluralism: An On-The-Spot History* to his wife with the kind words "To Lucy for putting up with my inability to deal with email." It is only one of many instances where the old and respected guard was unable to make the effort of staying up-to-date. Indeed, I have many friends like Sandler who pride themselves for not participating in what they call "This modern folly of the Internet that will not last," not realizing to what point they belittle themselves with such prehistoric comments.

And yet: in spite of the breathtaking speed of technological developments in the age of cyber space, it was never more important for us to turn our view back and reflect about those many generations of human beings before us, during which enormous lapse of time our given bodies and brains have evolved to become what they are today.

Could the search for that equilibrium between mind and body be an explanation why sexually explicit art has become such a successful recurring theme? Or is it simply the easy way out for many artists to take advantage of the fact that so many people are sexually frustrated and go to museums and art galleries where they are officially permitted to see naked bodies?

I believe more than ever that, as modern humans, we must find a sound balance between our minds that are floating in cyberspace and our bodies that are tied to mother earth.

I am also increasingly saddened about how primitive our basic day-to-day language has become, as characterized by the word "fuck," which has now entered the routine vocabulary of otherwise cultured people. This is true not only for America, but also around the entire globe, where this particular English expression has

31

become integrated in many of the world's leading languages.

Not to talk about Hollywood, where the four letter words and foul language have become a distinguished symbol of quality for want-to-be progressive filmmakers. Regrettably, those vulgarities have also found their way into our museums and art galleries.

Personally, I have distinct feelings of disgust when boundaries of erotic expression and aesthetic laws are broken by entering the field of the gutter. In my mind, such is not art. Please let there be no misunderstanding: I am not against sex, quite the contrary, but in my opinion foul language is not sexy.

A Fifteen Year Old Prophecy

Is there going to be a Renaissance, a re-thinking of our human condition, a stepping back to the essentials of survival and longing for happiness? In my opinion, the timing is overdue, and this all the more, as technological innovation has reached almost every aspect of our daily lives.

From 1993 to 1997, I worked on an art installation with Dr. Alan Peters, Associate Professor of Electrical Engineering in the Department of Electrical Engineering and Computer Science at Vanderbilt University: I called it *Project Mysterialism* and it was to be an art project that combined paintings and sculptures of traditional materials and techniques with then state of the art computer technology. In 1997, Dr. Peters and I wrote a paper about it, which - fifteen years later - appears to be every bit as up-to-date and valid as it was then. Here are some excerpts:

"Human society is at a juncture where certain questions become inevitable. Who are we? Where are we? Where are we going? Much might be learned by asking. "Where do we come from?" Yet, the answer provided by history in the conventional sense is inadequate. We stand at the end of a chain of eighty thousand generations of human beings. Can we derive insight, if not direct answers, to these questions through a regressive exploration of that chain? Direct exploration of ancient generations is not possible. However, our bodies, our senses are the same as our ancestors'. We must use our senses primordially and understand their true complexity, rather than accept at face value the modern trappings with which we are continually bombarded.

"It is perhaps ironic: the highest of technology coupled with the most primitive of sensory experience might lead us to that understanding. Modern technology permits the artist virtually to manipulate reality, to so completely control an environment that the viewer is estranged. Subtle ideas can emerge, no longer masked by the onslaught of mundane existence. Estrangement may be necessary to confront these questions, to be awestruck by the sublime reality of life itself. If the artist's environment moves the viewer emotionally back down the ancestral chain, the viewer may become aware of the closeness of his or her connection to all other people through the commonality of ancestry. Such an intuitive understanding of the kinship of humanity may be necessary to overcome the hatred and violence that plague society."

Background Reflections

"Have we illusions of who we are? Have we decided from experience that that which motivates human beings is greed, lust, jealousy and preservation - at any cost to others - of acquired privileges?

"We pride ourselves on the progress of modern civilization from its humble beginnings in the Tigris and Euphrates basin to its complete domination of the planet. We consider ourselves knowledgeable, even wise, after years of institutional education. We impress ourselves with the idea that the knowledge of humankind has doubled every fifteen years over the past century.

"Our generic inheritance fans out exponentially. The genes in one person today were assembled from those of 1,024 people ten generations past. Over a period of 500 years the genes of a million people become the pool for one person. In fact, recent studies of mitochondrial DNA suggest that all people share a common ancestor. If that is true, every human being is blood-related to every other.

"Human beings, as a species, have existed for about 1.6 million years. This is about 200 times as old as the oldest records of civilization. The four thousand years of reasonably well-known history are but one quarter of one percent of the time of our existence. Our focus on the past, recent past, and near future seemingly blinds us to a much broader prospective of human history. Our focus is natural enough, given the duration of an individual life and the lack of information about existence before a few thousand years ago."

3. The World as a Powder Keg

Demographic Explosion

At around 10,000 BC the estimated world population stood at about 1 million. By year 0 it had grown to around 100 million, and in 1900 it reached 1.65 billion. From 1950 to 2008 the world population exploded from 2.5 billion to 6.7 billion. And all of this in spite of two murderous World Wars and hundreds of bloody regional conflicts and genocides that killed over a hundred million people.

One of the contributing factors was life expectancy, which back in the Roman Empire stood at 22-25 years. Even by 1900, worldwide life expectancy was no greater than 30 years. Today, it stands at around 64, and in 2001, the US life expectancy was 74 for men and 80 for women.

More importantly, according to the Population Reference Bureau, the average age of the world's population stands only around 24 years. In other words: Half the world's population was not even born in 1985, and therefore cannot personally relate to any historic event that took place before that time. Does this explain why history keeps repeating itself?

Religious Conflicts

It is sad to say, but we have come no further than at the times of the religious crusades, almost a thousand years ago. Today, about 30 murderous armed conflicts continuously rage around the world, most of which are never even reported in any of our "breaking news" stories, for lack of monetary interest and reporters on the spot. 90 percent of those deadly wars involve Islamic extremists.

Islamic fascists and power-hungry dictators are willing to spare no blood to achieve their despicable goals of domination and oppression. They are living proof of how thin the varnish of our lauded human civilization really is, of how little it takes to expose and let lose the brutal animal underneath.

When paired with our presently simmering worldwide economic crises, such extreme will to power has historically led to wars. Sadly, today, there are all too many potential powder kegs around the world, be it the Middle East, North Korea, China, Pakistan, India, Iran or Russia. Any of those have the potential to explode into a major nuclear and worldwide conflict at any given moment, and this without even mentioning global viral epidemics.

Why do I include such a seemingly far-fetched analysis in this book about the Dada-Gene? Because life doesn't happen out of context, its aspects are interrelated.

4. Dada: An Answer to the World We Live In

In 1916, when Dada was born, Europe was in shambles. It was the middle of World War I and the dead soldiers were piling up on the battlefields. The whole world seemed to become unhinged. Amidst all the turmoil, a number of international refugees from the War met in Zurich/Switzerland to form the original Dada-Group at Cabaret Voltaire. The bourgeoisie, the banks and the industrialists, along with all their institutions (including museums) were blamed for these horrors.

The Dada artists came to the conclusion that the best answer to all this would be to become nonsensical.

Today, almost a hundred years later, we live in a world of turmoil again, and the artistic answer to the permanent smart talk may well be a similarly resounding "Dada!" Indeed, we have come again to live in un-chartered territories with countless "experts" claiming to know the answers, while, in fact, there are so many unanswered questions that nobody can honestly predict where the world economy and the desired peace process among the peoples are heading.

I wrote a poem about it:

To Sum It Up

The future looks a little hazy,
As our world is going crazy
And clicks away in cyberspace
Where our bodies lose their face.

The demographics are exploding
And our dollar is eroding
The rich get richer, that's for sure,
But our middle class stays poor.

Amidst that general confusion
Why don't you draw the wise conclusion
That rather than to clinch your fist
Convert, become a Dadaist!!

PART II: THE DADA MOVEMENTS

Chapter 3

The Beginning of Dada

1. Magic of the DADA Sound

The word DADA has magic. It is an early utterance of many of the world's children on the five continents. Its primitive sound can also be traced back to the cradle of many languages, including references to philosophical and even quasi-religious themes.

Dada is one of those sounds that evoke fascination. Drop the word in front of a cultured circle and you will be amazed how your friends start telling you about their personal experience and knowledge of the subject.

There is barely a culture, or language, around the world that doesn't include a Dada sound in one form or another:

- In English it means "father"
- In French it stands for "hobby horse"
- In German the word suggests "good bye," "get off my back," "be seeing you sometime"
- In Swiss German it means "here I am"
- In Russian and other Slavic languages it is "yes, yes"
- In India the word stands for "Godfather" in a Mafia sense,
- Etc., etc.

Indeed, since the beginning of the Dada movement, in 1916, Dada has never ceased to tickle the minds and influence the art- and literary worlds in one way or another.

Here's what some of the Dada artists themselves said about the word (from various internet sources):

- "Dada is beautiful, like the night that cradles the young day in her arms." - *Hans Arp*
- "DADA speaks with you, it is everything, it envelops everything, it belongs to every religion, can be either victory or defeat, it lives in space and not in time." - *Francis Picabia*
- "Dada is the sun, Dada is the egg. Dada is the Police of the Police." - *Richard Huelsenbeck*

Here is a quote from Merriam-Webster's Encyclopedia of Literature about Dada:

"Dada or Dadaism [French, from dada, child's word for a horse] Nihilistic movement in the arts that flourished chiefly in France, Switzerland, and Germany from about 1916 to about 1920 … and that was based on the principles of deliberate irrationality, anarchy, and cynicism and the rejection of laws of beauty and social organization. The most widely accepted account of the movement's naming concerns a meeting held in 1916 at Hugo Ball's Cabaret (Café) Voltaire in Zürich, during which a paper knife inserted into a French-German dictionary pointed to the word dada; this word was seized upon by the group as appropriate for their anti-aesthetic creations and protest activities, which were engendered by disgust for bourgeois values and despair over World War I."

Personally, I disagree with the above characteristic of "*...the rejection of laws of beauty.*" While, indeed, the Dadaists did proclaim such rejection of the laws of beauty, their artistic creations were definitely not bare of a sense of beauty and harmony in their compositions.

It is true that the original Dadaists had many internal fights and tensions among themselves when it came to defining their own movement. Moreover, pure nonsensical behavior tends to raise suspicions about the intellectual capacity of the perpetrator, who naturally risks to be branded as a "loser" in real life.

The common belief of the Dadaists was that focusing on the meaning rather than on the sound of words was at the root of many problems arising from political debates, which led to many conflicts and animosities. By contrast, the Dada poet was primarily sounding out words like a child, rather than becoming concerned with their meanings.

2. New York 1913: Cradle of Dada

Before the name Dada was even born, Marcel Duchamp (1887-1968) had anticipated its attack on traditional ideas. During World War I, the French native was living in New York and worked on a series of "ready-made" art objects, which gained him wide admiration for his commonplace and junk objects, including snow shovels, urinals and hat racks.

The first work by Marcel Duchamp that provoked significant controversy in 1912 was *Nude Descending a Staircase, No. 2.* The painting shows actually no resemblance with a nude, but supposedly depicts the idea of a mechanized nude in motion, thus simulating somehow the effects of a motion picture. It contains elements of fragmentation and cubist synthesis. Its movement and dynamism also remind of the "Futurists," an artistic and social movement that originated in Italy in the early 20th century.

Duchamp first submitted the piece to the Cubist "Salon des Indépendants" in Paris, but was forced to voluntarily withdraw it before the opening of the salon. In 1913, Duchamp showed that same painting in the New York *Armory Show*, which was officially named the *International Exhibition of Modern Art*. It was the first major exhibition of modern trends coming out of Paris. American visitors to the show, accustomed to realistic art, were scandalized.

"A few years after his arrival in the United States, Marcel Duchamp,…published three small and very short lived issues of what can only be described as genuine Dada-journals: The Blind Man No.1 (April 17…); The Blind Man No.2 (May 1917…) and Rongwrong(July 1917…). Of the three, the Blind Man No.2 is best remembered for publishing documents surrounding the scandal of Duchamp's 1917 urinal Fountain. But the other numbers also hold an abundance of material on the budding, European-infiltrated and subversive New York art scene." (Collections, TOUT FAIT: The Marcel Duchamp Studies Online Journal, vol. 1/ Issue3, December 2000, page 1)

Francis Picabia (1879-1953) was also a Frenchman who lived in New York during the First World War. He was an artist, writer and "bon vivant" who contributed to various art movements in the 20th century and became best known as a leader of Dada in Paris. From 1913 to 1915, Picabia took an active part in the avant-garde movements that introduced modern art to America.

The years of 1913-15 are known as Picabia's "Proto-Dada period," during which he mainly produced his "portraits mécaniques," a radically new style of painting based on curious machines. Most of them were symbolic of man and human activities, since Picabia believed that machines had become the point of reference of the modern world, and that man had created machines in his own image.

Even after the official kick-off in Zurich in 1916, New York continued to be a focal point of the Dada movement, more specifically at Alfred Stieglitz's Gallery 291, where Picabia had an important exhibition.

Traveling between the United States and Europe, Picabia became a link between the Dada groups in New York City, Zurich and Paris.

Hans Richter talks about his meetings with Picabia: "I met Picabia only a few times; but every time was like an experience of death. He was very strange, very magnetic, challenging and intimidating at the same time. All of us seemed to have moments when we temporarily felt the need to obey the anti-life impulse so virulently expressed by Picabia. I remember the moments of despair, caused by the war, by the injustice and stupidity of it all..." (Hans Richter: Dada Art and Anti-Art, Thames & Hudson Ltd., London, 2004, p. 74)

Picabia's Dada periodical *391* gained international fame, and from 1917 through 1924 it was published in Barcelona, New York City, Zurich and Paris. Its title emanated from his periodical 391 from Alfred Stieglitz's New York periodical *291*.

The American born <u>Man Ray</u> (1890-1976) was a friend of both Picabia and Duchamp and another big name of the New York Proto-Dada era. A multi-media painter and photographer, he became a co-founder with Duchamp and Katherine Dreier of the *Société Anonyme* in 1920, which became the first museum of modern art in the United States.

3. Zurich 1916: Official Beginning

Cabaret Voltaire was the name of a nightclub in Zurich, Switzerland, where the Dada Movement started in the midst of World War I, when a few refugees from that global conflict got together in Zurich, Switzerland, then a neutral country in the midst of armed conflicts. Among the many refugees coming to Zurich were artists from all over Europe.

It was the time of revolutionary ideas, with Vladimir Lenin living amongst them. It was a nihilistic, anti-art and anti-bourgeoisie movement that promoted the absurd, while the main idea behind it was "Form over Substance," in an environment where substance had become meaningless ("...The greatest prostitute was reason" - André Masson, 1924)

On February 5, 1916, the Dada Movement was officially founded by Hugo Ball (1886-1927), a German actor, artist and playwright, and his wife, the German performer and poet Emmy Hennings (1885-1948) as a cabaret for artistic and political purposes. Other founding members were the Romanian-born painter and architect Marcel Janco (1895-1984), the German poet, writer and drummer Richard Huelsenbeck (1892-1974), the Romanian artist and writer Tristan Tzara (1896-1963) and the German-French sculptor, painter, poet and abstract artist Jean Arp (1886-1966).

Ball and Hennings struck a deal with Ephraim Jan, patron of the *Holländische Meierei*, to use the back room of the cabaret for their own events. In 1915, the front had already hosted Zurich's first literary Cabaret, the *Pantagruel*.

The press release of February 2nd, 1916, which accompanied the opening of the nightclub, reads as follows:

"Cabaret Voltaire. Under this name a group of young artists and writers has been formed whose aim is to create a center for artistic entertainment. The idea of the cabaret will be that guest artists will come and give musical performances and readings at the daily meetings. The young artists of Zurich, whatever their orientation, are invited to come along with suggestions and contributions of all kinds. -Zurich, February 2, 1916" **Cabaret Voltaire (Zurich).**

In a reaction to the release, Hugo Ball describes the event: "The place was full to bursting; many could not get in. About six in the evening, when we were still busy hammering and putting up Futurist posters, there appeared an oriental-looking deputation of four little men with portfolios and pictures under their arms, bowing politely many times. – They introduced themselves: Marcel Janco the painter, Tristan Tzara, George Janco and a fourth, whose name I did not catch. Arp was also there, and we came to an understanding without many words. Soon Janco's opulent Archangels hung alongside the other objects of beauty and, that same evening, Tzara gave a reading of poems, conservative in style, which he rather endearingly fished out of the various pockets of his coat." (**Richter, p. 16**)

It was an overnight sensation in Zurich.

Hans Richter remembers that period of time: "To understand the climate in which Dada began, it is necessary to recall how much freedom there was in Zurich, even during a world war. The Cabaret Voltaire

played and raised hell at No.1, Spiegelgasse. Diagonally opposite, at No.12, Spiegelgasse, the same narrow thoroughfare in which the Cabaret Voltaire mounted its nightly orgies of singing, poetry and dancing, lived Lenin. Radek, Lenin and Zinoviev were allowed complete liberty. I saw Lenin in the library several times and once heard him speak at a meeting in Berne. He spoke good German. It seemed to me that the Swiss authorities were much more suspicious of the Dadaists, who were after all capable of perpetrating some new enormity at any moment, than of these quiet, studious Russians... even though the latter were planning a world revolution and later astonished the authorities by carrying it out."
(Richter, p. 16)

In June of 1916, Ball published a journal under the name of *Dada Manifesto*. It featured works from artists such as the poet Guillaume Apollinaire (1880-1918) and had a cover designed by Jean Arp.

The soirées at Cabaret Voltaire were often ruthless events, as artists experimented with new forms of performance, including simultaneous poetry and sound poetry.

Mirroring the turmoil of World War I, which was raging on Switzerland's borders, the art exhibited at the cabaret was often chaotic and brutal, with the audience even attacking the stage on at least one occasion.

Chapter 4

Dada Spreading

1. How Dada Was Spreading

Before the end of World War I, Tzara had become Dada's main promoter and manager, helping the Swiss group establish branches and "Dada Presidents" in other European countries. The international movement, which had originated in New York and Zurich at the height of the First World War, now spread to Berlin, Cologne, Hanover, and Paris, Romania and, to some extent, Russia.

While the Cabaret Voltaire in Zurich was the birthplace of the Dadaist movement, it also featured artists from every sector of the avant-garde scene, including Futurism's Filippo Marinetti (1876-1944) who, in 1918, founded the *Partito Politico Futurista,* or *Futurist* Political Party, which only a year later was absorbed into Benito Mussolini's *Fasci di Combattimento*, making Marinetti one of the first supporters and members of the Italian Fascist Party.

Influenced by the Zurich Dada movement, a number of radically experimental artists went on to change their artistic disciplines, like Wassily Kandinsky, Paul Klee, Giorgio de Chirico and Max Ernst.

Tzara inspired many young modernist authors from outside Switzerland to affiliate with the group, in particular the Frenchmen Louis Aragon, André Breton,

Paul Éluard, Georges Ribemont-Dessaignes and Philippe Soupault. Hans Richter, who came into contact with Dada at this stage in its history, notes that: "Dada was not a school of artists, but an alarm signal against declining values, routine and speculation, a desperate appeal on behalf of all forms of art, for a creative basis on which to build a new and universal consciousness of art." (Richter: p. 49)

In 1917, Tzara and Ball opened a permanent exhibition in Zurich under the name of *Galerie Dada*, through which they came in contact with the independent Italian visual artist Giorgio de Chirico (1888-1978) and with the German Expressionist journal *Der Sturm*, all of whom were described as *"fathers of Dada."*

During the same months, and probably owing to Tzara's intervention, the Dada group organized a performance of *Sphinx and Strawman*, a puppet play by the Austro-Hungarian Expressionist Oskar Kokoschka (1886-1980), which was advertised as an example of Dada Theater. Tzara was also in touch with *Nord-Sud*, the magazine of the French poet Pierre Reverdy (1889-1960), who attempted to unify all avant-garde trends and contributed articles on African art to both *Nord-Sud* and Pierre Albert-Birot's *SIC* magazine.

In a strict sense of the word, Dada never was a real movement, but rather a loose brotherhood of individual artists - mainly writers - who each had his or her own understanding of the word Dada. This is part of the reason why its different subchapters in various countries became unstable almost from the beginning and lost their influence as a group, which was going to lead to the follow-up movement of Surrealism.

2. Dada in Germany

Berlin

In early 1918, through the initiative of Richard Huelsenbeck, the Zurich Dadaists established contacts with their more explicitly left-wing disciples in Berlin: George Grosz, John Heartfield, Johannes Baader, Kurt Schwitters, Walter Mehring, Raoul Hausmann, Carl Einstein, Franz Jung, and Heartfield's brother Wieland Herzfelde.

Unlike their Zurich colleagues, who were insulting the European bourgeoisie as paper tigers from a secure location, the Berlin Dada movement of 1918 had a real revolution at hand. As Hans Richter recalls:

"There was the sound of firing in the streets and on the rooftops. Not only art, but all thought and all feeling, all of politics and society, had to be drawn into Dada's sphere of influence...While in one corner of Berlin, sailors were defending the imperial stables against troops loyal to the Kaiser, the Dadaists were laying their plans in another corner. When the stables fell, there was fighting at the Anhalter Bahnhof, in the Belle-Alliance-Platz and in Charlottenburg. Soldiers' councils and workers' councils, meetings, fraternal unions - a new age had dawned! Dada felt called upon to put the new age in perspective - and the old one out of joint." (Richter, p. 101)

In February 1918, Huelsenbeck delivered his first "Dada Speech" in Berlin, in which he attacked Expressionism, Futurism, Cubism, and abstract art in general. He claimed that Dada was defeating all these art forms. Simultaneously he hailed the writings of countless manifesto as the one literary form into which all feelings and thoughts could be compressed.

Cologne

Max Ernst (1891-1976) and his newlywed Lou Straus created a center for social activism in their Cologne apartment. Together with Jean Arp, Theodor Baargeld and Alfred Grünwald, they formed the new art movement "Dada Cologne." Lou's Dada name was "Armada Duldgedalzen." The group was greatly influenced by Marxism and Sigmund Freud's psychoanalysis.

Far away from the daily occurrence of firing squads and the assassination of Liebknecht and Rosa Luxemburg - as happened in Berlin - the atmosphere in Cologne was a lot less politically charged. Neither Max Ernst, nor his young painter friend Theodore Baargeld, wanted to use the Dada movement for political propaganda purposes. Still, they published a pro-communist periodical by the name of *Der Ventilator* (The Ventilator), meaning to blow some fresh air into the political climate by attacking Church, State, and the art establishment. The publication proved to be very successful.

Financial support for the *Ventilator* and its successor, *Die Schammade*, came from Baargeld's father, a powerful banker in Cologne, who was very thankful to Max Ernst and Jean Arp for converting his son from Pro-Communism to the more apolitical ideas of Dadaism.

Their first exhibit at the Cologne Art Society ended tumultuously and their posters and catalogues were confiscated. After that experience, they arranged the second exhibition in a backspace behind the men's room of a Cologne beer bar.

The German Dadaists, including Kurt Schwitters and Raoul Hausmann, particularly liked the technique of photomontage, using illustrations and advertisements, which they cut out of popular magazines. The Dadaists adapted the Cubist idea of collage to new purpose, that of making puzzling or strikingly incongruous juxtapositions of images and letters.

Hannover

A single name stands out in the Hannover Dadaist art scene: that of Kurt Schwitters. His famous collages were chiefly made of litter, bus tickets, sweet wrappings and other scrap objects. He was constantly traveling to spread the Dada idea, including visits to Switzerland, France, Holland, Norway, England and Czechoslovakia.

3. Dada in France

In late 1919, Tristan Tzara left Switzerland to join André Breton, Soupault and Claude Rivière to edit the Paris-based magazine *Littérature*. Already a mentor for the French avant-garde, Tzara was perceived as "Anti-Messiah" and a "prophet."

Around 1919, Tzara met American author and patron of the arts Gertrude Stein (1874-1946), who wrote about him, in *The Autobiography of Alice B. Toklas.* He also became involved in a number of Dada experiments, on which he collaborated with Breton, Aragon, Soupault, Picabia and Paul Éluard. Other authors who came into contact with Dada at that stage were Jean Cocteau, Paul Dermée and Raymond Radiguet.

Richter describes the relationship between writers and visual artists as follows:

"Paris Dada, unlike the Zurich, New York, Berlin, Hanover and Cologne movements, belonged almost exclusively to writers, not to visual artists... Painters were involved in the metaphysical revolt of the writers, but the visual medium could not, by its very nature, give form to pure protest. ...Insofar as they were artists, their work was art, however great their enthusiasm for anti-art." (Richter, pp.170-171)

The performances staged by Dada were often meant to popularize its principles, and Dada continued to draw attention on itself by hoaxes and false advertising, announcing - among others - that the Hollywood film star Charlie Chaplin was going to appear on stage at its show, or that its members were going to have their heads shaved, or their hair cut off on stage.

Dada activities in Paris culminated in March 1920 at the variety show at the Théâtre de l'Œvre, which featured readings from Breton, Picabia, Dermée and Tzara's earlier work, *The First Heavenly Adventure of Mr. Antipyrine*. Tzara's melody, "*Symphonic Vaseline*," which required ten or twenty people to shout "cra" and "cri" on a rising scale, was also performed. A scandal erupted when Breton read Picabia's "*Cannibal Manifesto*," lashing out at the audience and mocking them, to which they answered by throwing rotten fruit at the stage.

In 1922, the so-called "Congress of Paris" was an attempt to put an end to a power struggle between the different factions of the Dada movement. To no avail! Richter remembers: "Dada was approaching a crisis to which there was no solution. The whirlpool it had itself set in motion now sucked it under." (Richter, p.186)

4. How the Various Dada Movements Fell Apart

In May 1922, "a few Dadaists - Doesberg, Arp, Tzara, Schwitters and Richter met for a farewell to Dada in Weimar, where they attended a festival of the Bauhaus art school. Tzara delivered the funeral oration, which he later also took to Jena and Hanover, and Schwitters printed it in his periodical *Merz* as *Conference sur la fin de Dada.*

"Dada marches on, destroying more and more, not in extension but in itself... What interests a Dadaist is the way he himself lives...Dada is a state of mind...

"Dada is useless, like everything else in life...Dada is a virgin microbe which penetrates with the insistence of air into all those spaces that reason has failed to fill with words and conventions." **(Richter, p.191)**

The sad truth is that so many artists are egomaniacs who join a movement only to further their own visibility and cause, or -worse- to dominate the entire group. This is the chief reason why the different Dada movements in various countries came to an end, and why so many attempts to create permanent Dada movements survived only for short periods of time.

The initial Zurich group begun to dismantle shortly after the Big War ended in 1918, with its major actors going back to their original countries: Germany, France, Holland, Italy and the United States, where they created what they called "Dada subsidiaries."

In the end, the Dada Movement probably died because its initial ideas became corrupted. Like with every good idea, human greed took over, and Dada became institutionalized in a number of countries, with fights about leadership erupting among its initial members.

In his *Lecture on Dada*, in 1924, Tzara said: "Dada is a state of mind. That is why it transforms itself according to races and events. Dada applies itself to everything, and yet it is nothing, it is the point where the yes and the no and all the opposites meet, not solemnly in the castle of human philosophies, but very simply at street corners, like dogs and grasshoppers."

(Chipp, Herschel B.: *Theories of Modern Art.*University of California Press, Berkeley, Los Angeles and London, 1968, p. 389)

Chapter 5

Dada and Surrealism

1. Dream Art: Ancestor of Surrealism

Human fantasies and surreal art have been around for centuries, dating back as far as the Egyptian and Greek cultures in their depictions of gods and demons. In the Middle Ages, the Dutch painter Hieronymus Bosch (ca. 1450–1516) became a forerunner and model for the great artists of the Surrealist Movement, in particular Salvador Dalí (1904–1989).

In literature, the French Renaissance writer, doctor and humanist François Rabelais (c.1494–1553) is historically regarded as a major poet of fantasy, satire and the grotesque.

The strict doctrine of the medieval Catholic Church listed libido (the sexual desire) as "original sin." The only way to release artistic fantasies onto a canvas, and for the public to be able to indulge in it, was to depict sexually more or less explicit images by associating them to the devil.

Francisco de Goya (1746-1828), in his later years, did a series of paintings that he called "disasters of wars," using a similar approach a century later. In 1819, he painted the famous work *Saturn Devouring His Son* as another surreal and cruel interpretation of Roman mythology.

In the 20th century, Yves Tanguy, René Magritte and Salvador Dalí continued on that path. They are well known for the realistic depictions of dream imagery.

2. From Dada to Surrealism

The Dada and Surrealist movements have become a major part of 20th century art history. Dada began as an anti-art faction or, at least, a movement against the way art was appreciated by what was considered the civilized world, while the follow-up movement of Surrealism continued Dada's subversive attack on rational and "civilized" standards.

Most of the original Dada artists became the future leaders of the Surrealist movement. While Dadaism was, to a large extent, based upon the written word, the follow-up Surrealist époque was primarily dominated by painting and based in particular upon the dream world that had entered human consciousness in the wake of Sigmund Freud's psycho-analysis.

A more cynical mind might suggest that the uniquely painted or sculpted surreal art pieces attracted more collectors than the printed works of even the most creative writers, thus creating a greater monetary incentive for the Surrealist painters.

André Breton (1896-1966) and Marcel Duchamp (1887-1968) became the leading forces associated with Surrealism, the movement that dominated European painting in the 1920s and 1930s. At the beginning of the Dada movement, in 1916, Andre Breton had been too young to play a central role among its leaders. But later he became the driving force behind the passage from Dadaism to the Surrealist movement. Many of the Dada artists followed Breton's leadership and his pioneering spirit into the Surrealist movement as an extension of the Dada ideas.

Born in Normandy, Breton had studied medicine and psychiatry, and during World War I worked at a neurological clinic in Nantes. In 1919, he founded the *Revue Littérature* with Louis Aragon, and in 1924 was instrumental in the founding of the *Bureau of Surrealist Research.*

As André Breton states: "In the Surrealist Manifesto, I explained the circumstance that had originally put us, my friends and myself, on the track of the surrealist activity...The word *surrealism* having thereupon become descriptive of the generalizable undertaking to which we had devoted ourselves, I thought it indispensable, in 1924, to define this word once and for all:

"Surrealism, n. Pure psychic automatism, by which it is intended to express, verbally, in writing, or by other means, the real process of thought. Thought's dictation in the absence of all control exercised by the reason and outside all aesthetic or moral preoccupations."
(Chipp, pp.410-412)

The Surrealist Manifesto was written with a great deal of absurdist humor, thereby demonstrating the influence of the Dada movement.

Signers of the manifesto included Louis Aragon, Antonin Artaud, Jacques Baron, Joe Bousquet, Jacques-André Boiffard, Jean Carrive, Rene Crevel, Robert Desnos, Paul Éluard, Max Ernst, and, of course, André Breton.

Under Breton's direction, surrealism became a European movement that influenced all domains of the arts. One of its main ideas was to call into question the origin of human understanding and human perceptions of things and events.

During the *First International Congress of Writers for the Defense of Culture*, which opened in Paris in June of 1935, Breton had an open conflict with the Russian born Ilya Ehrenburg (1891-1967), the communist ideologue who later became the leading Soviet propagandist of World War II. In a pamphlet that said, among other things, that surrealists were pederasts (homosexuals), Ehrenburg insulted Breton and his fellow surrealists, whereupon Breton slapped Ehrenburg several times on the street. This, in turn, led to surrealists being expelled from the Congress.

1938, Breton accepted a cultural commission from the French government to travel to Mexico, where he met Trotsky, Diego Rivera and Frida Kahlo. Together, Breton and Trotsky wrote the manifesto *Pour un art révolutionnaire indépendent* (published under the names of Breton and Diego Rivera), which called for "complete freedom of the arts."

Throughout the 1930s, Surrealism continued to become more visible to the public at large. A Surrealist group developed in Britain. According to Breton, their 1936 London International Surrealist Exhibition was a high water mark of the period and became a model for international exhibitions. Surrealist groups in Japan, and especially in Latin America, the Caribbean and in Mexico produced innovative and original works. In 1929, Dalí joined the Surrealist group and helped shape the visual style between 1930 and 1935. Surrealism, as a movement, had found a method of its own. By exposing "psychological truth," they stripped ordinary objects of their inherent significance and created compelling images that were beyond ordinary formal organization and perception. Their images evoked empathy, laughter, outrage and bewilderment.

Max Ernst, who had already moved to Paris in 1921, was one of the first artists to join the pioneers of the Surrealist movement. As a former student of philosophy and psychology, he was particularly interested in the alternative realities experienced by the insane.

*

Three other names, too great to be contained by Surrealism, or to be left out here, come to mind: Picasso, Klee and Miró. They all produced Surrealist work, but remained somewhat aloof from the movement. Joan Miró, Paul Klee and André Masson practiced what they called the *Automatic Drawing Technique,* which is in line with my own *Dada Gut (or Dream) Drawings* that I have attributed to the activation of my Dada-Gene. Like in these Dada drawings, the line of the pen was allowed to rove at will without any conscious planning. Masson tried to achieve the same sort of result in painting, by drawing a mass of lines in an adhesive substance on the canvas, adding color by coatings of differently colored sand.

After the end of the Surrealist epoch, the approach of the *Automatic Drawing Technique* was carried into painting by Arshile Gorky (1904-1948) in New York, the *White Writing* paintings of Mark Tobey (1890-1976) and, above all, the vast abstractions of Jackson Pollock (1912-1956), in which he was almost drawing with paint, while working in an ecstatic trance.

Chapter 6

Continued Dada Attempts

The sound of the word *Dada* has evoked so much fascination over time that to this very day there have been continued attempts to revive the term by applying it to a number of different art movements. The most important was Neo-Dada.

1. Neo-Dada

In the 1950s, a number of young artists were eager to escape the dominance of *Abstract Expressionism*. They introduced a new label by the name of *Neo-Dada*, a term that was primarily applied to the visual arts, describing artwork that had similarities in method or intent to the initial Dada movement. The artists often used modern materials and popular imagery, but with absurdist contrast. They also denied traditional concepts of aesthetics.

The term of *Neo-Dada* was later popularized by Barbara Rose in the 1960s, but referred primarily to a group of artworks created in the 1950s and 1960s.

Neo-Dada, however, never really took off as a movement and gave way to what is now better known as *The New York School.*

Today, Neo-Dada is considered a rather transitional phase that was leading onto Pop Art, which also attacked the concept of Modernism. It was the idea that "art exists on a higher plane than mundane everyday life and focuses instead on the creation of a visual philosophy or spirituality that would lead humankind to a better future."(www.cartage.org.lb/en/themes/arts/painting/.../neodada.htm)

By the 1950s, many of the younger artists had become disillusioned, after they found that the Modernist dream had failed in spite of all the rhetoric. The world had not changed, nor created a higher "spiritual reality."

*

One of the most prominent artists of the Neo-Dada movement was Robert Rauschenberg (1925-2008) who opened the door for many artists since 1960 to challenge the Modernist view of painting and sculpture. He believed that all aspects of life were open to art.

Rauschenberg never worked in a typical style for a prolonged period of time, which explains why some critics accused his work of being jumpy and eclectic. Much of his work was based on the basic cultural assumption that a work of art can be executed in any material, from a stuffed goat to a live human body, and in any physical environment: on a stage, in front of a TV camera, underwater, on the surface of the moon, or in a sealed envelope. It also can fit any purpose, including contemplation, amusement, invocation, or threat. And it can be found in any possible environment: from the museums to a trashcan.

Rauschenberg was just a single name of an impressive list of international artists who at one time or another associated their names with the term of Neo-Dada. That list of Neo-Dadaists includes the following names:

Joseph Beuys, Lee Bontecou, John Chamberlain, Bruce Conner, Jim Dine, Mark Divo, Richard Hamilton, Jasper Johns, Allan Kaprow, Andy Kaufman, Edward Kienholz, Yves Klein, Robert Morris, Claes Oldenburg, Yoko Ono, Nam June Paik and, indeed, Robert Rauschenberg.

Yet, "Some critics simply regarded the Neo-Dadaists as satirical rather than for or against anything." (Hapgood, Susan: *Neo-Dada – Redefining Art 1958-62.* American Foundation of Arts, 1994 – p.12)

Throughout the 20th century, the Dada idea never died as Hans Richter remembers: "…these new Pop-people have chosen Marcel Duchamp as their patron saint and placed him in an honored niche. But Marcel Duchamp escaped from this niche very quickly. In a letter dated November 10th 1962, he (Duchamp) writes to me:

"This Neo-Dada, which they call New Realism, Pop Art, Assemblage, etc., is an easy way out, and lives on what Dada did. When I discovered ready-mades, I thought to discourage aesthetics. In Neo-Dada they have taken my ready-mades and found aesthetic beauty in them. I threw the bottle-rack and the urinal into their faces as a challenge, and now they admire them for their aesthetic beauty." (Richter, pp. 207-208)

According to another source, however, Richter had to admit years later that the above quote was actually not directly "straight from a letter written to him by Duchamp," but first emanated from Richter who had sent the paragraph to Duchamp for comment, and simply received Duchamp's approval in return, written into the margins as "OK, ça va très bien" (OK, that's very good).
(ToutFait.com: The Marcel Duchamp's On-Line Journal – updated 02/25/05)

2. Manifestomania

Parallel to the revival of the Dada idea by the Neo-Dadaists in the visual art, the written manifestos re-surfaced in a number of renewed contexts. "Manifestomania" in the arts started with Filippo Tommaso Marinetti's *Futurist Manifesto* of 1909 and was followed by Hugo Ball's *Dada Manifesto* of 1916, which was rewritten in 1918 by Tristan Tzara.

Tzara summed up the writing of manifestos in the following words: "To put out a manifesto, you must want A B C and fulminate against 1 2 3." (Tzara Manifesto 1918)

Soon, many artists wanted to publish their own manifestos, each proclaiming to come up not only with new ideas, but also to be "the best."

In 1930, the *Concrete Art Manifesto* ("Art is Universal") was published, and the *Manifesto of Mural Painting* followed in 1933. The list goes on and on, including the *White Manifesto* of 1946, the *Spatialist Manifesto* of 1952, the manifestos offered by the *Situationists* (1960), *Chelsea Hotel* (1962), *Fluxus* (1963), *SCUM* (1967) *Body Art* (1975), *Cheap Art"* (1984) and many more.

In 1999, as a counter-current, some young British artists published the *Stuckist Manifesto* (Stuck, stuck, stuck) to protest "dominance of conceptual art, at the expense of figurative painting." This manifesto was *a 20-point manifesto*, "against conceptualism, hedonism and the cult of the ego artist." It stated that "Art that has to be in a gallery to be art, isn't art," and that "Stuckism is anti-ism."

So why then a manifesto? Mr. Thomson, promoter of Stuckism, put it this way: "It's a bit like poetry. It compresses feelings and thoughts in a memorable form. You have to strike a chord with supporters, and make those who don't agree with you as angry as possible."

While Marinetti had to buy newspaper space, the Stuckists have spread their ideas free of charge via the Internet. Today, they count 187 groups in 45 countries, the latest being the *Tehran Stuckists*. "But it's not like joining a cult," says Mr. Thomson. "We encourage people to write their own version of the manifesto; if you want to be a Stuckist you have to do it yourself, and the only way to leave is to throw yourself out of your own group." (www.stuckism.com)

And where did the father of the "art Manifestomania," Marinetti, end up? He spent his life writing hundreds of futurist manifestos: on painting, film, music, noise, women, men's clothing, lust, the future reconstruction of the universe; and even food, where he called for the abolition of pasta.

3. Being an Artist: A Harsh Profession

In the 1950s, the New York scene of serious artists was confined to no more than a few hundred names, and everybody knew everybody else. Today, there are many hundred art galleries in Manhattan alone, and the number of artists is in the tens of thousands.

Many artists today come from wealthy families; yet, the majority of the serious artists are less fortunate: they struggle to make a living. While many pursue other activities to pay for their life as artists, others have chosen what I would call "the easy way out" by painting sexually explicit works. It is barely a satisfactory artistic enterprise, but from a monetary standpoint it makes sense: In 2006, worldwide porn revenues were estimated at $97 Billion dollars.

In the 1950s and 60s, the Neo-Dadaists of the New York School chose the more genuine approach of becoming revolutionaries, as they tried to abolish all leftovers of traditional values. But the "ruling class" smiled upon them, bought up their works for pennies, filled our museums with their art, and - over the next 50 years - jacked up the prices of a single piece to the insane levels of tens of millions of dollars.

As for the early lives of the New York Neo-Dada artists, they had been living in extreme poverty for the longest period. They raised rent money through "spaghetti parties" and were saved by Franklin Roosevelt's *New Deal* in 1933, as my late painter friend Vito Migliore remembered. Then, one day, some of them got rich beyond their wildest dreams. It took them so much by surprise that they became alcoholics, drug addicts, and some even committed suicide.

*

Being an artist myself, I understand that urge of always pushing ahead, never standing still, constantly on the move to create new horizons. Unfortunately, that is also the worst recipe for making money. I have a European artist friend who specializes in drawing vague love scenes, somehow erotic, but without being sexually explicit or pornographic. He has been doing it for over twenty years, sells like crazy all over the world, and makes tons of money.

4. Dada Today

The word Dada has never ceased to tickle the imagination of people in a myriad of forms, from children, to casual family talk, to the visual arts, to writing and to the musical world. As previously mentioned here, I was stunned to find myself in company with 56.8 million Internet surfers!

Isn't that living proof that its magic is more alive today than ever?

Chapter 7

The Dada Greats

A Fresh Look At Their Life Histories

Biographies tend to become sequences of statistical data, from which the blood and flesh of the subject has been removed. So much has been written about the major Dada artists that writing another set of biographies would be unwarranted for the purpose of this book.

As an artist and fellow Dadaist myself, I feel encouraged to sketch a few biographical outlines and revive some of their personal stories, as reported by contemporary eyewitnesses at the time, some of which may have been forgotten through the passage of time by their scholarly biographers.

My hope is to bring a bit of their souls and individualities back to life, among the otherwise dry description of events and numerical data. I found Hans Richter to be the most helpful source of such colorful accounts.

For the above reasons, the biographies (in alphabetical order) of the following "Dada Greats" are not meant to be comprehensive by any account.

Guillaume Apollinaire (1880-1918)

Wilhelm Albert Włodzimierz Apolinary Kostrowicki, known as Guillaume Apollinaire, was a French poet, writer and art critic. He was born in Italy to a Polish noblewoman born near Navahrudak (now in Belarus). Apollinaire's father is unknown, but may have been Francesco Flugi d'Aspermont, a Swiss-Italian aristocrat who disappeared early from Apollinaire's life.

Kostrowicki was partly educated in Monaco. When he later immigrated to France, he adopted the name Guillaume Apollinaire.

Apollinaire was one of the most popular members of the artistic community of Montparnasse in Paris. His friends and collaborators during that period included Pablo Picasso, Gertrude Stein, Max Jacob, André Salmon, Marie Laurencin, André Breton, André Derain, Faik Konica, Blaise Cendrars, Pierre Reverdy, Jean Cocteau, Erik Satie, Ossip Zadkine, Marc Chagall and Marcel Duchamp. In 1911, he joined the Puteaux Group, a branch of the cubist movement.

Apollinaire's first collection of poetry was *L'enchanteur pourrissant* (The decaying enchanter - 1909), but *Alcools* (1913) established his reputation. The poems, influenced in part by the Symbolists, juxtapose the old and the new, combining traditional poetic forms with modern imagery. In 1913, Apollinaire published the essay *Les Peintres cubistes* on the cubist painters, a movement that he helped to define. He also came up with the term *Orphism* to describe a tendency towards absolute abstraction in the paintings of Robert Delaunay and others.

Apollinaire fought in World War I where, in 1916, he endured a serious shrapnel injury to his temple. While recovering from this wound, he wrote *Les Mamelles de Tirésias*. During that same period, he invented the word *Surrealism* in the program notes for Jean Cocteau and Erik Satie's *ballet Parade*, first performed on 18 May 1917. He also published an artistic manifesto, *L'Esprit nouveau et les poètes* (The new spirit and the poets).

Apollinaire's status as a literary critic became most famous and influential through his recognition of the Marquis de Sade, whose works had been obscure for a long time, yet arising in popularity as an influence upon the Dada and Surrealist art movements. It was part of all that was going on at Montparnasse, at the beginning of the twentieth century, as "The freest spirit that ever existed."

"The word *Surrealism*, thus invented by Apollinaire, was foremost used as a weapon to destroy Dada. When Breton states that he was a Surrealist, even when he was a Dadaist, this is perfectly true, as far as he personally is concerned."
(Richter, p. 193-194)

Who knows what destiny might have had in store for this outstanding man. But Apollinaire died too young, at the age of only 38. Two years after being wounded in the war, his weakened body did not survive the 1918 Spanish flu pandemic.

Apollinaire was interred at the *Le Père Lachaise* Cemetery, in Paris.

Jean Arp (1886-1966)

Jean Arp, also known as "Hans Arp," was a German-French sculptor, painter, poet and abstract artist in other media, including torn and pasted paper.

Arp was born in Strasbourg as the son of a French mother and a German father following the Franco-Prussian War. The Alsace area was then known as Alsace-Lorraine, Following the return of Alsace to France at the end of World War I. French law determined that his name *Hans* had to become *Jean*. Later, when Arp spoke in German, he referred to himself as "Hans", and when he spoke French, he called himself "Jean."

In 1904, after leaving the *École des Arts et Métiers* (Arts and Crafts) in Strasbourg, Arp went to Paris where he published his poetry for the first time.

From 1905 to 1907, Arp studied art at the Kunstschule in Weimar, Germany, and in 1908 went back to Paris, where he attended the Académie Julian.

In 1915, he moved to Switzerland, taking advantage of Swiss neutrality. He later told the story of how he had avoided being drafted into the army, when he was notified to report to the German embassy: On the paperwork he had been given, he wrote the date into the first blank space. He then wrote the date again in every following blank space, drew a line beneath them, and carefully added up all the numbers. Finally, he took off all his clothes and handed in his paperwork. Whereupon he was told to go home.

In 1916, Arp was one of the founding members of the Dada movement in Zurich. In 1920, after the end of World War I, he founded the Cologne Dada group in Germany, along with Max Ernst.

In 1925, after Dada had been funneled into Surrealism, his work also appeared in the first exhibition of the surrealist group at the Galerie Pierre in Paris.

In 1926 Arp moved to the Paris suburb of Meudon, and in 1931 he broke with the Surrealist movement and founded *Abstraction-Création* in Paris and the periodical *Transition*.

"In 1927 Arp received his first big commission to paint the interior of the Restaurant Aubette in Strasbourg, his hometown. He invited his wife Sophie and Theo van Doesburg to help him. They complemented each other, as Anti Art and Art had come together. This was no longer Dada but quite simply new art. The fruit of Dada!" (**Richter p. 197**)

Throughout the 1930s and until the end of his life, Arp wrote and published many essays and poems. In 1942, he escaped the French occupation and lived in Zurich until the end of the Second World War.

In 1949, Arp visited New York City for a solo exhibition at the Buchholz Gallery. Subsequently, he was commissioned to do a mural at the UNESCO building in Paris. In 1954, Arp won the Grand Prize for Sculpture at the Venice Biennale.

A retrospective of his work was held at the New York Museum of Modern Art in 1958, followed by a 1962 exhibition at the Musée National d'Art Moderne, in Paris, France.

After his first wife, the artist Sophie Taeuber-Arp, died in Zürich in 1943, Arp married the collector Marguerite Hagenbach.

Arp died in 1966, in Basel, Switzerland.

Hugo Ball (1886-1927)

Hugo Ball was the primary founder of the Dada movement in Zurich and one of its leading artists. He was a German author, poet and actor. Born in Pirmasens, Germany, he was raised in a Catholic family. He studied sociology and philosophy at the universities of Munich and Heidelberg (1906–1907), and, according to Coutts-Smith, tried to found an Expressionist theatre in Munich. In 1910, Ball moved to Berlin where he became an actor and collaborated with Max Reinhardt. His wife, Emmy Hennings, was also a poet and was dancing and singing at the "Café des Westens."

At the beginning of World War I, Hugo Ball joined the army as a volunteer, but after the invasion of Belgium got disillusioned, as in his opinion the war was founded on a glaring mistake and men had been confused with machines. Considered a traitor in his country, he immigrated to Switzerland with his wife, Emmy Hennings, who also became an important Dada personality. They settled in Zurich, where Vladimir Lenin was also living at the time. Ball continued his special interest in anarchism, particularly in Bakunin who had been a leading 19th century figure in the history of anarchism and an opponent of Karl Marx's idea of dictatorship of the proletariat. Ball worked on a book of Bakunin translations, which never got published. Although interested in anarchist philosophy, he nonetheless rejected it for its militant aspects, and viewed it as only a means to his personal goal of enlightenment.

In 1916, Hugo Ball wrote the "Dada Manifesto," making a political statement about his views on the terrible state of society and acknowledging his dislike for philosophies in the past, while claiming to possess the "ultimate truth."

That same year, Ball wrote his poem *Karawane*, which is a German poem consisting of nonsensical words. Its meaning resides in its meaninglessness, reflecting the chief principle behind Dadaism. Some of his other best known works include the poem collection *Seven Schizophrenic Sonettes*, a drama by the name of *The Nose of Michelangelo*, a memoir of the Zurich period named *Flight Out of Time, A Dada Diary,* a biography of Hermann Hesse entitled *Hermann Hesse - His Life and Work,* and, finally, K*ritik der deutschen Intelligenzia"* (Critique of the German Intelligentsia).

*

As co-founder of the Cabaret Voltaire in Zurich, Ball led the Dada Movement and is the main person credited with naming the movement *Dada*, by allegedly choosing the word at random from a dictionary. He later created the *abstract phonetic poem* as a new art form by chanting vowel sequences like a recitative, in liturgical style.

Hugo Ball's involvement with the Dada movement lasted about two years. The path that Tristan Tzara was leading the movement was "not for him" as he explained. "I have examined myself carefully, and I could never bid chaos welcome." (Richter, p 43)

He later worked for a short period as a journalist for the *Free Journal* in Bern. Eventually, he retired to the Swiss Southern Canton of Ticino where he lived a religious and relatively poor life until his death in 1927.

André Breton (1896-1966)

Breton was a commanding personality who became the driving force behind the passage from the Dadaists to the Surrealists. Born to a family of modest means in Tinchebray (Orne) in Normandy, Breton studied medicine and psychiatry. During World War I he worked in a neurological ward in Nantes, where he met Jacques Vaché, whose anti-social attitude and disdain for established artistic tradition influenced Breton considerably. Vaché committed suicide at age 24. His war-time letters to Breton and others were published in a volume entitled *Lettres de guerre* (1919), for which Breton wrote four introductory essays.

In *Les Champs Magnétiques* (The Magnetic Fields), together with Soupault, he put the principle of "automatic writing" into practice.

Automatic writing is a process of writing text that does not come from the conscious thoughts of the writer. Practitioners say that the writer's hand forms the message, with the person being unaware of what will be written. The approach is largely similar to what I call my own "Gut Writings." (See Chapter 9 Par. 6)

In 1924, Breton published the "Surrealist Manifesto" and that same year became the editor of *La Révolution surréaliste.* He also assembled a group around him, some of whom were former Dadaists: Philippe Soupault, Louis Aragon, Paul Éluard, René Crevel, Michel Leiris, Benjamin Péret, Antonin Artaud, and Robert Desnos. Breton said: "Our collective resistance to artistic or moral laws gives us only momentary satisfaction. We are very well aware that beyond and above this, a distinctive individual imagination is at work in each of us - and that this is more *Dada* than the movement itself." (Richter, p. 216)

Anxious to combine the themes of personal transformation found in the works of Arthur Rimbaud with the politics of Karl Marx, Breton joined the French Communist Party in 1927, from which he was expelled in 1933. He also had his own art gallery, which helped him to survive during those hard times by selling off paintings.

At the beginning of World War II, Breton enlisted again in the medical corps of the French Army. But when the Vichy government banned his writings as "the very negation of the national revolution," Breton escaped to the United States from where he travelled to the Caribbean in 1941. There, he met Martinican writer *Aimé Césaire*, and later wrote the introduction to the 1947 edition of Césaire's *Cahier d'un retour au pays natal.*

Breton married three times: His first wife (1921-1931) was the former Simone Kahn, and his second wife the former Jacqueline Lamba, with whom he had his only child, a daughter named Aube. He met his third wife, Elisa Claro - a Chilean woman - in 1944 during his exile in New York City. That same year, he and Elisa travelled to the Gaspé Peninsula in Québec, Canada, where he wrote *Arcane 17*, a book which expresses his fears of World War II, describes the marvels of the *Rocher Percé* (Pierced Rock) at the north-eastern end of North America, and his newly found love with Elisa.

After the War, Breton returned to Paris in 1946. He intervened against French colonialism (he was a signatory of the "Manifesto of the 121" against the Algerian war). From 1961 to 1965, he continued to promote a second group of surrealists by the name of *La Breche.* But the movement never made it big.

André Breton died in 1966 at age 70 and was buried in the Cimetière des Batignolles in Paris.

Salvador Dalí (1904-1989)

Salvador Domingo Felipe Jacinto Dalí i Domènech, was born on May 11, 1904, in the town of Figueres, Spain. Dalí's older brother, also named Salvador (born October 12, 1901), had died of gastroenteritis nine months earlier, on August 1, 1903. His father, Salvador Dalí i Cusí, was a middle-class lawyer and notary whose strict disciplinary approach was tempered by his wife, Felipa Domenech Ferrés, who encouraged her son's artistic endeavors. When he was five, Dalí was taken to his brother's grave and told by his parents that he was his brother's reincarnation, a concept which he came to believe.

Dalí also had a sister, Ana María, who was three years his minor. In 1949, she published a book about her brother, *Dalí As Seen By His Sister*.

Dalí attended drawing school. In 1916, he also discovered modern painting on a summer vacation to Cadaqués with the family of Ramon Pichot, a local artist who made regular trips to Paris. The following year, Dalí's father organized an exhibition of his charcoal drawings in their family home. Dalí had his first public exhibition at the Municipal Theater in Figueres in 1919.

In February 1921, Dalí's mother died of breast cancer when the boy was sixteen years old; he later remembers his mother's death as the greatest blow he had experienced. After her death, Dalí's father married his deceased wife's sister. Dalí did not resent this marriage, because he had a great love and respect for his aunt.

In 1922, Dalí moved into the Residencia de Estudiantes (Students' Residence) in Madrid and studied at the Academia de San Fernando (School of Fine Arts). Lean and 5 ft. 8 in. tall, Dalí already drew attention as an eccentric and dandy personality. He wore long hair and sideburns, coat, stockings, and knee breeches in the style of English aesthetes of the late 19th century. However, it was his paintings, in which he experimented with Cubism that earned him the most attention from his fellow students. At the time of these early works, Dali probably did not completely understand the Cubist movement. His only information on Cubist art came from magazine articles and a catalog given to him by Pichot, since there were no Cubist artists in Madrid at the time.

In 1924, the still-unknown Salvador Dalí illustrated his first book. It was a publication of the Catalan poem *Les bruixes de Llers* (The Witches of Llers) by his friend and schoolmate, the poet Carles Fages de Climent.

Dalí also experimented with Dada, which influenced his work throughout his life. At the Residencia, he became close friends with (among others) Pepín Bello, Luis Buñuel, and Federico García Lorca. The friendship with Lorca had a strong element of mutual passion, but Dalí fearfully rejected the erotic advances of the poet.

Dalí was expelled from the Academia in 1926, shortly before his final exams, when he stated that "no one on the faculty was competent enough to examine him". (artzia.com/history/biography/dali)

That same year, he made his first visit to Paris, where he met Pablo Picasso, whom the young Dalí revered. Picasso had already heard favorable reports about Dalí from Joan Miró. As he developed his own style over the next few years, Dalí painted a number of works heavily influenced by Picasso and Miró.

Certain trends in Dalí's work that would continue throughout his life were already evident in the 1920s. Dalí devoured influences from many styles of art, ranging from the most academically classic to the most cutting-edge avant-garde. His classical influences included

Raphael, Bronzino, Francisco de Zurbaran, Vermeer, and Velázquez. He used both classical and modernist techniques, sometimes in separate works, and sometimes combined. Exhibitions of his works in Barcelona attracted much attention, along with mixtures of praise and puzzled debate from critics.

Dalí grew a flamboyant moustache, influenced by seventeenth-century Spanish master painter Diego Velázquez. The moustache became an iconic trademark of his appearance for the rest of his life.

In 1929, Dalí collaborated with surrealist film director Luis Buñuel on the short film *Un chien andalou* (An Andalusian Dog). His main contribution was to help Buñuel write the script for the film. Also, in August 1929, Dalí met his inspiration, and future wife Gala, born Elena Ivanovna Diakonova. She was a Russian immigrant eleven years his senior, who at that time was married to surrealist poet Paul Éluard. That same year, Dalí had important professional exhibitions and officially joined the Surrealist group at the Montparnasse quarter of Paris. The Surrealists hailed what Dalí called the Paranoiac-critical method of accessing the subconscious for greater artistic creativity.

Meanwhile, Dalí's relationship with his father was close to rupture. Don Salvador Dalí y Cusi strongly disapproved of his son's romance with Gala, and saw his connection with the Surrealists as a bad influence on his morals. The final event that broke the relationship was when Don Salvador read in a Barcelona newspaper that his son in Paris had exhibited a drawing of the *Sacred Heart of Jesus Christ* with the provocative inscription, "Sometimes, I spit for fun on my mother's portrait."

Outraged, Don Salvador demanded from his son to recant publicly. Dalí refused, perhaps out of fear of expulsion from the Surrealist group, and was violently thrown out of his paternal home on December 28, 1929. His father told him that he would disinherit him, and that he should never set foot in Cadaqués again. Dalí later claimed that, in response, he handed his father a condom containing his own sperm, saying, "Take that. I owe you nothing anymore!"

(http://antinewworldorder.blogspot.com/2009/03/salvador-dali.html)

The following summer, Dalí and Gala rented a small fisherman's cabin in a nearby bay at Port Lligat. He bought the place, and over the years enlarged it, gradually building his much beloved villa by the sea.

In 1931, Dalí painted one of his most famous works, *The Persistence of Memory*, which introduced a surrealist image of soft, melting pocket watches. The general interpretation of the work is that the soft watches are a rejection of the assumption that time is rigid or deterministic. This idea is supported by other images in the work, such as the wide expanding landscape, and the other limp watches, shown being devoured by insects.

Dalí and Gala, having lived together since 1929, were married in 1934 in a civil ceremony. They later remarried in a Catholic ceremony in 1958.

Dalí was introduced to America by art dealer Julian Levy in 1934. The exhibition in New York of Dalí's works, including Persistence of Memory, created an immediate sensation. Manhattan socialites celebrated him at a specially organized "Dalí Ball." He showed up wearing a glass case on his chest that contained a bra. That same year, Dalí and Gala attended a masquerade party in New York, hosted for them by heiress Caresse Crosby. For their costumes, they dressed as the Lindbergh baby and its kidnapper. The resulting uproar in the press was so great that Dalí had to apologize. When he returned to Paris, the Surrealists confronted him about his apology for a surrealist act.

While the majority of the Surrealist artists had become increasingly associated with leftist politics, Dalí maintained an ambiguous position on the subject of the proper relationship between politics and art. He insisted that surrealism could exist in an apolitical context and refused to explicitly denounce fascism. Among other factors, this had landed him in trouble with his colleagues. Later in 1934, when he was formally expelled from the Surrealist group, it is said that Dalí replied, "I myself am surrealism."

*

Hans Richter quotes Dali from his 1929 declaration, which Richter characterizes as the most precise description of Dada: "Surrealism is the systematization of confusion. Surrealism appears to create an order, but the purpose of this is to render the idea of system suspect by association. Surrealism is destructive, but it destroys only what it considers to be shackles limiting our vision." (Richter, p. 194)

In 1936, Dalí took part in the London International Surrealist Exhibition. His lecture, entitled *Fantomes paranoiques authentiques*, was delivered while wearing a deep-sea diving suit and helmet. He had arrived carrying a billiard cue and leading a pair of Russian wolfhounds. He had to have the helmet unscrewed as he gasped for breath. His comment was that he just wanted to show that he was plunging deeply into the human mind.

At this stage, Dalí's main patron was the very wealthy British poet Edward James who had helped Dalí to emerge into the art world by purchasing many works and by supporting him financially for two years. They became good friends, and James is featured in Dalí's painting *Swans Reflecting Elephants*. They also collaborated on two of the most enduring icons of the Surrealist movement: the *Lobster Telephone* and the *Mae West Lips Sofa*.

In 1940, as World War II was raging in Europe, Dalí and Gala moved to the United States, where they lived for eight years. After the move, Dalí returned to the practice of Catholicism.

Dali wrote a novel, published in 1944, about a fashion salon for automobiles. This resulted in a drawing by Edwin Cox in The Miami Herald, depicting Dalí dressing an automobile in an evening gown. Also in *The Secret Life*, Dalí suggested that he had split with Buñuel because the latter was a Communist and an atheist. Buñuel was fired (or resigned) from MoMA, supposedly after Cardinal Spellman of New York went to see Iris Barry, head of the film department at MoMA. Buñuel then went back to Hollywood, where he worked in the dubbing department of Warner Brothers from 1942 to 1946. In his 1982 autobiography *Mon Dernier soupir* (My Last Sigh, published 1983), Buñuel wrote that, over the years, he rejected Dalí's attempts at reconciliation.

Starting in 1949, Dalí spent his remaining years back in his beloved Catalonia. The fact that he chose to live in Spain while it was ruled by Franco drew criticism from progressives and from many other artists.

*

Late in his career, Dalí did not confine himself to painting, but experimented with many unusual or novel media and processes: he was among the first artists to employ holography in an artistic manner. Several of his works incorporate optical illusions. In his later years, young artists such as Andy Warhol proclaimed that Dalí had an important influence on pop art.

Dalí's post-World War II period bore the hallmarks of technical virtuosity and an interest in optical illusions, science and religion. He became an increasingly devout Catholic, but suffered a deep shock by the destruction of Hiroshima and the *dawning of the atomic age*. Dalí labeled this period "Nuclear Mysticism." In paintings such as *The Madonna of Port-Lligat* (first version of 1949) and *Corpus Hypercubus* (1954), Dalí sought to synthesize Christian iconography with images of material disintegration, inspired by nuclear physics. *Nuclear Mysticism* included such notable pieces as *La Gare de Perpignan* (1965) and *Hallucinogenic Toreador* (1968–70). In 1960, Dalí began working on the *Dalí Theatre and Museum* in his home town of Figueres; it was his largest single project and the main focus of his energy through 1974. He continued to make additions through the mid-1980s.

In 1980, Dalí's health took a catastrophic turn. His near-senile wife, Gala, allegedly had been dosing him with a dangerous cocktail of none-prescribed medicine that damaged his nervous system, thus causing an untimely end to his artistic capacity. At age 76, Dalí was a wreck, and his right hand trembled terribly with Parkinson-like symptoms.

In 1982, King Juan Carlos of Spain bestowed on Dalí the title Marquis of Púbol, for which Dalí later repaid him with his drawing *Head of Europa*, which would turn out to be Dalí's final drawing, after the king visited him on his deathbed.

Gala died on June 10, 1982. After Gala's death, Dalí had lost much of his will to live. He deliberately dehydrated himself, possibly as a suicide attempt, or maybe in an attempt to put himself into a state of "suspended animation," as he had read some microorganisms can do. He moved from Figueres to the castle in Púbol, which he had bought for Gala and was the site of her death. In 1984, a fire broke out in his bedroom under unclear circumstances. It may have been another suicide attempt by Dalí, or simple negligence by his staff. In any case, Dalí was rescued and returned to Figueres, where a group of his friends, patrons, and fellow artists saw to it that he was comfortable living in his Theater-Museum in his final years.

There have been allegations that Dalí was forced by his guardians to sign multiple blank canvases that would later, even after his death, be used in forgeries and sold as originals. As a result, art dealers tend to be wary of late works attributed to Dalí.

On January 23, 1989, while his favorite record of Tristan and Isolde played, he died of heart failure at Figueres at the age of 84, and, coming full circle, is buried in the crypt of his Teatro Museo in Figueres. The location is across the street from the church of Sant Pere, where he had his baptism, first communion, and funeral, and is three blocks from the house where he was born.

Marcel Duchamp (1887-1968)

Duchamp was born in Blainville-Crevon, Seine-Maritime, in the Haute-Normandie region of France, into a cultured family that enjoyed such activities as chess, reading books and playing music together.

The following three of his siblings also became successful artists:
- Jacques Villon (1875-1963), painter, printmaker
- Raymond Duchamp-Villon (1876-1918), sculptor, and
- Suzanne Duchamp-Crotti (1889-1963), painter.

Duchamp spent seven years at the Lycée Corneille in Rouen. Though he was not an outstanding student, he won two mathematics prizes at the school. He also won a prize for drawing in 1903, when he decided to become an artist. He took drawing and academic drawing classes from a teacher who unsuccessfully attempted to protect his students from Impressionism, Post-Impressionism and other avant-garde influences.

However, Duchamp's true artistic mentor was his brother Jacques Villon, whose fluid style he sought to imitate. At 14, his first serious art attempts were drawings and watercolors, depicting his sister Suzanne Duchamp in various poses and activities. That summer he also painted landscapes in an Impressionist style, using oils.

Duchamp experimented with classical techniques and subjects, as well as with Cubism and Fauvism. Later, when asked about what had influenced him most at the time, Duchamp cited the work of the Symbolist painter Odilon Redon, whose approach to art was somehow anti-academic and notably individual.

From 1904 to 1905 he studied art at the *Académie Julian*, but preferred playing billiards rather than attending classes. During this time Duchamp drew and sold humorous cartoons. Many of the drawings used visual and/or verbal puns. Such play with words and symbols would engage his imagination for the rest of his life.

In 1905, Duchamp worked for a printer in Rouen. There, he learned the typography and printing processes - skills he would use in his later work.

Thanks to his brother, Jacques Villon's membership in the prestigious *Académie royale de painture et de sculpture*, Duchamp's work was exhibited in the 1908 *Salon d'Automne* for the first time. The following year his work was featured in the *Salon des Independants.* Of his pieces in that show, Guillaume Apollinaire criticized what he called "Duchamp's very ugly nudes." Nevertheless, the two of them later became close friends.

Duchamp also started a life-long friendship with Francis Picabia, after meeting him at the 1911 *Salon d' Automne.* It was Picabia who introduced Duchamp to a lifestyle of "fast cars and high living."

In 1911, the Duchamp brothers hosted a group of other artists and writers at Jacques Villon's home in Puteaux. The guests included Picabia, Robert Delaunay, Fernand Léger, Roger de la Fresnaye, Albert Gleizes, Jean Metzinger, Juan Gris, and the Russian artist Alexander Archipenko. The group came to be known as the *Puteaux Group*, and the artists' works were dubbed "Orphic Cubism."

Uninterested in the Cubists' seriousness or in their focus on visual matters, Duchamp did not join in discussions of Cubist theory, which gained him a reputation of being shy. However, later that year he did paint in a Cubist style and added an impression of motion by using repetitive imagery.

During this period, Duchamp's fascination with transition, change, movement and distance became manifest and, like many artists of the time, he was intrigued with the concept of depicting a "fourth dimension" in art. Works from this period included his first "machine painting," *Coffee Mill (Moulin à café* -1911), which he gave to his brother Raymond. The *Coffee Mill* shows similarity to the "grinder" mechanism of the piece *Large Glass*, which he was to paint years later.

His 1911 *Portrait of Chess Players (Portrait de joueurs d'echecs)* shows the Cubist overlapping frames and multiple perspectives of his two brothers playing chess, to which Duchamp added elements conveying the unseen mental activity of the players. (The French word "échec," meaning "chess" is also French for "failure.")

The first work by Marcel Duchamp that provoked significant controversy was *Nude Descending a Staircase, No. 2 (Nu descendant un escalier n° 2* - 1912), which he had to take back from the *Salon des Independants.* He submitted that same painting to the 1913 *Armory Show* in New York City, which was organized by Alfred Stieglitz. It was officially named the *International Exhibition of Modern Art*, which was the first major art exhibition of modern trends coming out of Paris. American show-goers, accustomed to realistic art, were scandalized, and the *Nude* was at the center of much of the controversy.

After that, Duchamp increasingly left "retinal art" behind. At that time he had read Max Stirner's *The Ego and Its Own,* the study of which he considered another turning point in his artistic and intellectual development. The essence of the book is that *ego is always there in everything.*

He was also fascinated by the stage adaptation of Raymond Roussel's 1910 novel *Impressions d'Afrique,* which featured plots that turned in on themselves, word plays, surrealistic sets, and humanoid machines.

Duchamp later acknowledged that Roussel's drama radically changed his approach to art, and that it inspired him to begin the creation of his *Bride Stripped Bare By Her Bachelors, Even* (later often called *The Large Glass)*. Duchamp was reportedly working on the piece from 1915 to 1923, with the exception of periods in Buenos Aires and Paris from 1918 - 1920. He executed the work on two panes of glass with materials such as lead foil, fuse wire and dust. It combines chance procedures, plotted perspective studies and laborious craftsmanship.

After 1912, Duchamp painted few canvases, and in those he did, he tried to remove "painterly" effects, using instead a technical drawing approach.

During this decade, Duchamp worked as a librarian at the *Bibliotèque Sainte-Geneviève* to earn his living. He withdrew from painting circles into a scholarly environment, while studying math and physics - areas in which exciting new discoveries were taking place.

Duchamp's own art-science experiments began during his tenure at the library. To make one of his favorite pieces, *3 Standard Stoppages* (*3 stoppages étalon*), he dropped three 1-meter long threads onto prepared canvases, one at a time, from a height of 1 meter. After the threads landed in three random undulating positions, he varnished and fixed them on to blue-black canvas strips, before attaching them to glass. He then cut three wood slats into the shapes of the curved strings and put all the pieces into a box.

*

In 1914, after the declaration of World War I, Duchamp felt uncomfortable in Paris. While his brothers and many of his friends had joined the army, Duchamp got himself exempted. He decided to immigrate to the then-neutral United States. In 1915, to his surprise, he found that he was already a celebrity when he arrived in New York. Here, he befriended art patron Katherine Dreier and artist Man Ray. Duchamp's circle included art patrons Louise and Walter Conrad Arensberg, actress/ artist Beatrice Wood and Francis Picabia, as well as other avant-garde personalities. He spoke little English, but quickly learned the language while supporting himself by giving French lessons and through library work.

For two years, the Arensbergs were the landlords of his studio, and they would remain his friends and patrons for 42 years. In lieu of rent, they agreed that his payment would be *The Large Glass*. An art gallery offered Duchamp $10,000 per year in exchange for all of his annual production, but Duchamp declined the offer, preferring to work on *The Large Glass*.

The New York Dada Movement had a less serious tone than the one of European Dadaism and was not a well-organized venture. Duchamp's friend Picabia connected with the Dada group in Zurich, bringing to New York the Dadaist ideas of absurdity and "anti-art." A group met almost nightly at the Arensberg home, or caroused in Greenwich Village. Together with Man Ray, Duchamp contributed his ideas and humor to the New York activities. They also worked on the concept of "found art."

Richter writes: "The ready-made was the logical consequence of Duchamp's rejection of art and of his suspicion that life was without a meaning. He exhibited to a public of connoisseurs a single bicycle wheel mounted on a stool, a bottle-rack... and, finally, a urinal. He declared that these ready-mades became works of art as soon as he said they were. When he "chose" this or that object, a coal shovel for example, it was lifted from the limbo of un-regarded objects into the living world of works of art: looking at it made it into art!" (Richter, p.88)

*

The most prominent example of Duchamp's association with the New York Dada-Movement was his 1917 submission of the F*ountain* urinal to the Society of Independent Artists. Artworks in the *Independent Artists* shows were not selected by jury, but rather all pieces submitted were displayed. However, the show committee insisted that *Fountain* was not art, and rejected it from the show. This caused uproar amongst the Dadaists and led Duchamp to resign from the board of the *Independent Artists*.

Along with Henri-Pierre Roché and Beatrice Wood, Duchamp published a Dada magazine in New York, entitled *The Blind Man*, which included art, literature, humor and commentary.

After World War I, when Duchamp returned to Paris, he did not participate in the Dada group. In 1919, Duchamp made a parody of the *Mona Lisa* by adding a moustache and goatee to a cheap reproduction of the painting. To this he added the rude inscription *L.H.O.O.Q.*, a pun which, when read out loud in French, sounds like *"Elle a chaud au cul,"* which translates as "She has a hot ass," implying that the woman in the painting is in a state of sexual excitement and availability. It may also have been intended as a Freudian joke, referring to Leonardo da Vinci's alleged homosexuality.

Duchamp's interest in kinetic works can be found as early as the notes for the two ready-mades: The Large Glass and the *Bicycle Wheel,* and despite losing interest in what he called "retinal art," he retained interest in visual phenomena. In 1920, with help from Man Ray, Duchamp built a kinetic sculpture, called *Rotative plaques verre, optique de precision* (Rotary Glass Plates, Precision Optics). The piece, which he did not consider to be art, involved a motor to spin pieces of rectangular glass on which were painted segments of a circle. When the apparatus spins, an optical illusion occurs, in which the segments appear to be closed concentric circles. (Animation of *Rotary Glass Plates)*

The next phase of Duchamp's spinning works were the *Rotoreliefs.* To make the optical play toys, he painted designs on flat cardboard circles and spun them on a phonographic turntable. When spinning, the flat disks appeared three-dimensional. He had a printer produce 500 sets of six of the designs, and set up a booth at a 1935 Paris inventors' show to sell them. The venture was a financial disaster, but some optical scientists thought they might be of use in restoring three-dimensional stereoscopic sight to people who had lost vision in one eye.

In essence, Duchamp was no longer a practicing artist. Instead, he played chess, which he studied for the rest of his life to the exclusion of most other activities.

In 1925, at the occasion of the Third French Chess Championship, he became a chess master. He also participated in the Olympiads from 1928-1933, favoring then hypermodern openings, such as the Nimzo-Indian.

The idea of the "endgame" is important to an understanding of Duchamp's complex attitude towards his artistic career. Irish playwright Samuel Beckett used the theme as the narrative device for his 1957 play of the same name, *Endgame*.

In 1942, Duchamp made New York's Greenwich Village his home. He advised modern art collectors and major museums, thereby helping to shape the taste of Western art during his lifetime.

From then until 1944, together with Max Ernst, Eugenio Granell and Breton, Duchamp edited the Surrealist periodical *VVV*, and also served as an advisory editor for the magazine *View*, which featured him in its March 1945 edition, thus introducing him to a broader American audience.

Duchamp married twice. In June 1927, he married the wealthy Lydie Sarazin-Lavassor. However, their marriage fell apart only six months later.

In 1954, he married Alexina "Teeny" Sattler and they remained together until his death. Duchamp became a United States citizen in 1955.

Duchamp's influence on the art world remained behind the scenes until the late 1950s, when he was "discovered" by young artists such as Robert Rauschenberg and Jasper Johns, who were eager to escape the dominance of Abstract Expressionism.

Duchamp's final major artwork surprised the art world, which believed he had given up art for chess 25 years earlier. Said piece is a picture, visible only through a peephole in a wooden door. A (not very pretty) nude woman can be seen lying on her back with her face hidden, legs spread, and one hand holding a gas lamp in the air against a landscape backdrop. From 1946 to 1966 Duchamp had reportedly worked in secret on the piece in his Greenwich Village studio, while even his closest friends thought he had abandoned art.

Huelsenbeck remembers the following words by Duchamp: "A painter is first of all not a painter, he has to distrust his senses, he has to know what he is doing first, and his task is to investigate not the reality, but the transcendental quality of the object. Doing this with artistic means is a mere coincidence."
(Huelsenbeck – Memoirs of a Dada Drummer, p. 114-115)

That same year the Tate Gallery hosted a large exhibit of his work. Other major institutions, including the Philadelphia Art Museum and the Metropolitan Museum of Art, followed with large showings of Duchamp's work. He was invited to lecture on art and to participate in formal discussions, as well as sitting for interviews with major publications.

Marcel Duchamp died on October 2, 1968 in Neuilly-sur-Seine, France, and is buried in the Rouen Cemetery, in Rouen, France. His grave bears the epitaph, *"D'ailleurs, c'est toujours les autres qui meurent;"* or "By the way, it's always the others who die."

*

Much has been written about this intriguing man who had such an influence on the 20th century art scene. He certainly was a faithful Dadaist who told his friend Richter that the Dada idea never died during his time.

"When I discovered ready-mades, I thought to discourage aesthetics." **(Richter, pp. 207-208)**

The theory that the creative act is not performed by the artist alone, but that the spectator brings the work in contact with the external world by deciphering and interpreting its "inner qualities," and thus adding his contribution to the creative act, flattered the collectors into the belief that they were part of the process, which contributed greatly to his commercial success.

96

In 2004, as a testimony to the legacy of Duchamp's work to the art world, his *Fountain* (Urinal), which he signed as "R. Mutt", was voted "most influential artwork of the 20th century" by a panel of prominent artists and art historians. (Note: The word *Armut* in German means "Poverty." Could this be a coincidence, like so many other word plays contained in his work titles?)

Max Ernst (1891-1976)

Max Ernst was a well-known painter, sculptor and writer, and a leading figure of the German Dadaist, the French Surrealist, as well as the American Abstract Expressionist movements of the 20th century.

He was born in Brühl, Germany, near Cologne. Max Ernst tells the following story (in the 3rd person): "Cologne lies at the very edge of a wine-producing region. Beer country lies to the North, wine country to the South. Are we the product of what we drink? If so, it may not be without significance that Max has always preferred wine…When in later life he reflected on the Thirty Years' War, it occurred to him that this was a war between beer-drinkers and wine-drinkers. Perhaps he was right…"

And later: "Little Max's first contact with painting was in 1894, when he watched his father painting a water color entitled *Loneliness*. There was a frightening stillness about the way in which it was depicted… "In 1896 little Max did a series of drawings, of his father, his mother, his sister Maria who was his elder by one year, himself, two younger sisters, Emmi and Luise…

"In 1897 first contact with the void: his sister Maria kissed him and her sisters goodbye and died a few hours later. Since this time, a feeling for Nothingness and destructive forces has been dominant in his temperament, in his behavior and - later - in his work.

"First contact with hallucinations: measles. Fear of death and destructive forces. A fever vision, inspired by a panel of imitation mahogany opposite the foot of his bed. The grain of the wood gradually took on the appearance of an eye, a nose, a bird's head, a 'menacing nightingale', a spinning top, and so on. It is certain that little Max enjoyed being plagued by such visions. And later he voluntarily induced similar hallucinations by staring at wooden panels, clouds, wallpaper and unpainted walls in order to allow his imagination free play. If someone asked him 'What do you like doing most of all?' he always answered 'looking'…

"First contact with occult and magical powers. One of his best friends, a highly intelligent and devoted pink cockatoo, died on the night of January 5, 1906. It was a fearful shock to Max when he found the dead bird next morning, at the same instant as his father informed him of the birth of his sister Lori. Such was the boy's perturbation that he fainted. In his imagination he connected the two events and blamed the baby for the bird's decease. A series of emotional crises and depressions followed. A dangerous confusion between birds and human beings took root in his mind and later found expressions in his drawings and paintings…Even later Max identified himself with *Loplop, the Superior of the birds.*" (Richter p.156-158)

*

After abandoning his study of philosophy and psychology at the University in Bonn, he began painting, but never received any formal artistic training, and thus was able to freely indulge in his fantasy world.

During World War I Ernst's artist career was interrupted, as he was called on duty to serve in the German army.

In 1913, Max Ernst had met Lou Straus together with his friend Jean Arp at an art class at the University of Bonn, where Lou studied Art History. They were married in 1918 against the will of both families, hers of Jewish background and his of catholic. In 1920, their son Hans-Ulrich, later known as the artist Jimmy Ernst, was born.

Max Ernst rediscovered a technique that was known in ancient China and by the old Greeks, which he called *Frottage*.

"In caves and on tombstones in China and ancient Greece there were mythological or historical scenes cut into the stone. By rubbing these through on to rice-paper or parchment, it was possible to obtain a negative impression.

"Max Ernst subjected this process to a refined process of development and perfected several methods of producing images and impressions which must be respected as his professional secrets." (Richter p. 163)

*

"In 1921 Ernst was to move to Paris. His temperament was such that, if there had been no Paris, it would have had to be built specially for him," as Hans Richter remembers that time. (Richter p. 161)

*

Max Ernst had joined fellow Dadaists André Breton, Gala (Dalí's later wife), Paul Éluard and Tristan Tzara at the artistic community of Montparnasse and became a surrealist painter, along with their new movement. The two conservative families, Ernst and Straus, broke with the eccentric pair and in 1926 Lou and Max were divorced.

In 1927, Ernst married Marie-Berthe Aurenche. It is thought that his relationship with her may have inspired the erotic subject matter of *The Kiss* and other works of that year. In 1930, he appeared in the film *L'Âge d'or*, directed by Luis Buñuel.

Together with Paul Klee, Max Ernst created paintings, prints and collages, and worked with mixed media. He also worked with Joan Miró on designs for Sergei Diaghilev. With Miró's help, Ernst pioneered grattage in which he troweled pigments from his canvases. He also explored with the technique of decalcomania, which involves pressing paint between two surfaces.

Ernst drew a great deal of controversy with his 1926 painting *The Virgin Chastises the infant Jesus before Three Witnesses*: André Breton, Paul Éluard, and the Painter.

In 1934, Ernst began his work as a sculptor and spent time with Alberto Giacometti.

In 1938, along with fellow surrealist Hans Bellmer, Ernst was interned in *Camp des Milles*, near Aix-en-Provence, where the French held many German and Austrian nationals as suspected spies. Thanks to the intervention of Paul Éluard and other friends, including the journalist Varian Fry, Ernst was discharged a few weeks later. Soon after the Nazi occupation of France, he was arrested again, this time by the Gestapo, but managed to escape and flee to America with the help of Peggy Guggenheim. The US heiress and patron of the arts acquired a number of Max Ernst's works, which she displayed in her new museum in London. Ernst and Guggenheim arrived in the United States in 1941 and were married the following year.

During the Second World War, Lou Ernst-Straus had moved to France. Max and their son Jimmy had tried to get her an exit visa to America, with the help of Eleanor Roosevelt, but tragically she was deported on one of the last trains to Auschwitz in 1944 and was never heard of again.

Ernst's marriage to Peggy Guggenheim did not last. In October 1946, in a double ceremony with Man Ray and Juliet P. Browner, he married Dorothea Tanning in Beverly Hills, California. The couple then made their home in Sedona, Arizona.

"Paris never lost its hold on him. He did succeed in escaping from occupied France to America, but he could never settle down there. His sharp and delicate wit was out of place as a weapon against American directness. They saw only the morbid side of his imagination, and wanted none of it. He withdrew to Arizona, where an inescapable Indian element still lingers in the landscape. There he created fabulous sun-pictures and lunar landscapes, some of them vest-pocket size (Microbes). He surrounded his house with evil, spectral sculptures, until he was able to go back to France. He was welcomed like a long-lost son. Then, at last, New York remembered him and honored him...with a big exhibition at the Museum of Modern Art.

"Max Ernst's work was rightly described as Dadaist until 1923. From 1924 onwards, thanks solely to the word-magic of André Breton, it turned *Surrealist* without really changing at all." (Richter, p. 164)

In 1948, Ernst wrote the treatise *Beyond Painting,* which was a great success. As a result of the publicity, he started to become wealthy.

In 1953, Ernst and Tanning moved to a small town in the south of France where he continued to work. The *City* and the *Galeries Nationales du Grand-Palais* in Paris published a complete catalogue of his works.

Ernst died on April 1st , 1976, in Paris. He was interred there at the Père Lachaise Cemetery.

*

His son, Jimmy Ernst (1920-1984) was a prominent writer and a well-known German/American abstract expressionist-painter who lived on the south shore of Long Island. His memoirs, *A Not-So-Still Life*, render a fascinating account of 20th century European and American art history and were published shortly before his death.

Jimmy Ernst's daughter Amy and her brother Eric are both active artists and work in New York City and on Long Island.

*

In 2005, *Max Ernst: A Retrospective* opened at the Metropolitan Museum of Art and included works such as *Celebes* (1921), *Ubu Imperator* (1923), and *Fireside Angel* (1937), which is one of the few political pieces and is sub-titled *The Triumph of Surrealism,* depicting a raging bird-like creature that symbolizes the wave of fascism over Europe.

Richard Huelsenbeck (1892-1974)

Richard Huelsenbeck was a poet, writer and drummer born in Frankenau, Hesse-Nassau. On the eve of World War I he was a medical student. He then enlisted in the army, but in February 1916, after being invalided in the war, he immigrated to Zurich, Switzerland, where he joined the Dada Group at the Cabaret Voltaire.

Huelsenbeck became a prominent part of the Zurich and Berlin Dada movements. As an expressionist poet and writer he also became known as a war-protestor.

He returned to Berlin in January 1917, initiating the Dada group there, along the ideas and techniques of his former Zurich colleagues. Hugo Ball wrote of him, in his *Escape from Time,* on February 11, 1916: "Huelsenbeck has arrived. He pleads for an intensification of rhythm … He would best love to drum literature & to perdition."

*

In February 1918, Huelsenbeck delivered his "First Dada Speech" in Berlin. "This began with the statement that the meeting was a demonstration of solidarity with international Dadaism, the international artistic movement founded in Zurich two years before. He then launched a ferocious attack on Expressionism, Futurism and

Cubism, and heaped curses on abstract art, proclaiming that all these theories had been defeated by Dada. He ended with a reading from his *Phantastische Gebete* (Fabulous Prayers)." (Richter, p. 102-103)

In 1920 Huelsenbeck wrote: "To make literature with a gun in my hand had for a time been my dream." His ideas fitted in with the left-wing politics that were prevailing in Berlin at the time. However, the idealistic thoughts of Huelsenbeck and his companions, and their challenge of "Dada is German Bolshevism," had unfortunate consequences when the National Socialists denounced all aspects of modern art as "Kunst-Bolschewismus."

*

Later in life, Huelsenbeck moved to New York City, where he practiced C.G. Jung's psychoanalysis under his assumed name of "Charles R. Hulbeck."

In his autobiography *"Memoirs of a Dada Drummer,"* he writes: "The conflict between being a Dadaist and being a doctor has followed me all my life." (Huelsenbeck, *Memoirs of a Dada Drummer*, Viking Press, New York, 1969, p. 186)

Huelsenbeck was also the editor of the *Dada Almanach*, and wrote *Dada Siegt!* (Dada Victory*)*, *En Avant Dada* (Forward Dada!) and other Dadaist works. Until the end of his life, Huelsenbeck insisted, "Dada still exists." He was the most enthusiastic spokesman for Dada. Surprisingly, while he wanted to destroy art, he continued to paint.

In 1970 he returned to the Ticino region in Switzerland and died there in Muralto in 1974.

Marcel Janco (1895-1984)

Marcel Janco was a Romanian-born painter and architect, and one of the founders of the Dada movement. He was born to a Jewish family in Bucharest and was often found in company of his brothers Georges and Jules.

A friend and compatriot of Tristan Tzara, Janco was among the founders of the Dadaist movement at Cabaret Voltaire in Zurich.

*

"Like Tristan Tzara, Marcel Janco and his brothers had drifted to Zurich from Bucharest, the Paris of the Balkans. Before coming to Switzerland, Janco had been a hard-working and conscientious student of architecture. He had stored up everything in his memory, from the rush basket, Moses' portable dwelling for the first few days of his life, to Bramante's Studies in Harmony and Perspective and the Renaissance theories of Leone Battista Alberti. This was reflected in the abstract reliefs, which he produced and which soon hung on our walls," as Hans Richter remembers. (Richter, p.22-23)

Later, his artistic creations were influenced by the group's discovery that chance must be recognized as a new stimulus. Richter continuous: "Chance became our trademark. We followed it like a compass. We were entering a realm of which we knew little or nothing, but to which other individuals, in other fields, had already turned... Each man explored the new discovery in his own way. Janco used whatever discarded objects Nature happened to place in his path. These *objects trouvés* (found objects) he incorporated in abstract sculptures and reliefs of a new kind." (Richter p. 51 and 55)

In 1922, he returned to Romania and worked as an architect and painter, but he never forgot Dada and his friends. From time to time he sent a periodical from Bucharest, called *Contimporanul,* which he claimed was pursuing "Dada ideas into practical life," but as it was written in Rumanian, nobody could read it.

*

In 1941, Janco left Romania for Mandate Palestine to escape the Nazis. In 1953, Janco established the Ein Hod artists' village near Haifa, Israel. Towards the end of his life he helped found the Dada museum in Ein Hod which bears his name. The museum houses Janco's art, explores the history of Dadaism, and hosts exhibitions.

Janco died on April 21, 1984 at the age of 89.

Filippo Tommaso Marinetti (1876-1944)

Filippo Tommaso Marinetti was an Italian ideologue, poet, editor, and founder of the Futurist movement. A millionaire Italian poet with a passion for fast cars, he created an artistic movement out of nothing. He sat down and created his "-ism", Futurism, and then went about recruiting Futurist artists. It was an early exercise in cultural branding. Marinetti took over the front page of newspapers across Europe and had his manifesto printed - a sort of "advertorial for speed, youth, newness and the destruction of the old order."

In June of 1916, Marinetti was named as a contributor to the *Publication Cabaret Voltaire:* "Contributions: Apollinaire, Picasso, Modigliani, Arp, Tzara, van Hoddis, Huelsenbeck, Kandinsky, Marinetti, Cangiullo, van Rees, Slodki, Ball, Hennings, Janco, Cendrars etc." (Source: CHRONIQUE ZURICHOISE 1915 – 1919 - first page by Tristan Tzara, written in 1922)

Manifesto of Futurism

2009 marks the 100th anniversary of Marinetti *Futurist Manifesto*. When it initially appeared, on February 20, 1909, it was the first art manifesto of the 20th century, paving the way for the Dadaists and Surrealists.

Marinetti's Manifesto had to have 11 bullet points, because 11 was Marinetti's favorite number. Dr Roberta Cremoncini of London's *Estorick Collection of Italian Art* writes: "Marinetti sounds a bit mad, but was serious. He was a self-publicist, but wanted to change Italian culture too, to update it and break in a very clear way with the past. This is why the manifesto dictates burning museums, a cleansing war, to shake Italy."

Art critic William Feaver wrote: "Futurism came at a very good moment for getting excited about the 20th century. Bang at the beginning, just avoiding the start of the war. The manifesto was about publicity, he published to become famous. And they became famous."

Here is the text of the *Manifesto of Futurism*:

1. We want to sing the love of danger, the habit of energy and rashness.
2. The essential elements of our poetry will be courage, audacity and revolt.
3. Literature has up to now magnified pensive immobility, ecstasy and slumber. We want to exalt movements of aggression, feverish sleeplessness, the double march, the perilous leap, the slap and the blow with the fist.
4. We declare that the splendor of the world has been enriched by a new beauty: the beauty of speed. A racing automobile with its bonnet adorned with great tubes like serpents with explosive breath ... a roaring motor car which seems to run on machine-gun fire, is more beautiful than the Victory of Samothrace.
5. We want to sing the man at the wheel, the ideal axis of which crosses the earth, itself hurled along its orbit.
6. The poet must spend himself with warmth, glamour and prodigality to increase the enthusiastic fervor of the primordial elements.
7. Beauty exists only in struggle. There is no masterpiece that has not an aggressive character. Poetry must be a violent assault on the forces of the unknown, to force them to bow before man.

8. We are on the extreme promontory of the centuries! What is the use of looking behind at the moment when we must open the mysterious shutters of the impossible? Time and Space died yesterday. We are already living in the absolute, since we have already created eternal, omnipresent speed.

9. We want to glorify war - the only cure for the world - militarism, patriotism, the destructive gesture of the anarchists, the beautiful ideas which kill, and contempt for woman.

10. We want to demolish museums and libraries, fight morality, feminism and all opportunist and utilitarian cowardice.

11. We will sing of the great crowds agitated by work, pleasure and revolt; the multi-colored and polyphonic surf of revolutions in modern capitals: the nocturnal vibration of the arsenals and the workshops beneath their violent electric moons: the gluttonous railway stations devouring smoking serpents; factories suspended from the clouds by the thread of their smoke; bridges with the leap of gymnasts flung across the diabolic cutlery of sunny rivers: adventurous steamers sniffing the horizon; great-breasted locomotives, puffing on the rails like enormous steel horses with long tubes for bridle, and the gliding flight of airplanes whose propeller sounds like the flapping of a flag and the applause of enthusiastic crowds.

"Futurism was one of the main arsenals from which Dada drew its weapons." (Richter p. 216)

*

Marinetti spent the first years of his life in Alexandria, Egypt. His love for literature became evident when at seventeen he started his first school magazine, *Papyrus*. He went to a Jesuit school where he was threatened to be expelled for bringing Emile Zola's scandalous novels to classes.

He was sent to Paris, France, where he obtained his baccalaureate in 1893 and subsequently went to Italy to study law at the University of Pavia. After obtaining his degree in 1899, Marinetti decided to abandon law and follow his literary vocation. He experimented incessantly in every field of literature (poetry, narrative, theatre, words in liberty).

His *Futurist Manifesto* of 1909 was read and debated all across Europe, but Marinetti's first "Futurist" works were not as successful. In April, the opening night of *Le Roi Bombance* (The Feasting King), written in 1905, was interrupted by loud whistling on the part of the audience... and by Marinetti himself, who thus introduced another essential element of Futurism, "the desire to be heckled." Marinetti did, however, fight a duel with a critic he considered too harsh.

Even his drama *La donna è mobile* (The lady is flexible), presented in Turin, was not terribly successful.

In 1910, his first novel *Mafarka il futurista* was cleared of all charges in an obscenity trial. But that year, Marinetti would discover some unexpected allies when three young painters (Umberto Boccioni, Carlo Carrà, Luigi Russolo) decided to join the Futurist movement. Together with them (and with poets such as Aldo Palazzeschi), Marinetti launched a series of Futurist Evenings, theatrical spectacles in which the Futurists declaimed their manifestos in front of a crowd that, more often than not, attended the performances in order to throw vegetables at the Futurists.

In 1911, the Italo-Turkish War broke out and Marinetti departed immediately for Libya as war correspondent for a French newspaper. His articles were eventually collected and published in *The Battle Of Tripoli*.

In the meantime he worked on a violently anti-Catholic and anti-Austrian verse-novel, *Le monoplan du Pape* (The Pope's Aeroplane, 1912) and edited an anthology of futurist poets. But his attempts to renew the language of poetry did not satisfy him. So much so that in his foreword to the anthology, he launched a new revolution: it was time to be done with traditional syntax and to move towards "words in freedom" (parole in libertà).

Marinetti supported Italian intervention in World War I. In Milan, in September 1914, the Futurists, led by Marinetti, fought each other at a pro-war demonstration, and on a similar occasion in 1915 Marinetti was arrested together with the future Fascist leader, Benito Mussolini. Marinetti encouraged the Futurists to depict warlike subjects in their paintings. In July 1915, Marinetti volunteered for the Lombard cyclist's battalion, in which he was wounded and decorated for bravery.

Marinetti and Fascism

In early 1918, Marinetti founded the *Partito Politico Futurista* (Futurist Political Party), which only a year later was absorbed into Benito Mussolini's Fasci di combattimento, making Marinetti one of the first supporters and members of the Italian Fascist Party. He opposed Fascism later, calling it "reactionary," and walking out of the 1920 Fascist party congress in disgust.

However, throughout the Fascist regime, Marinetti sought to make Futurism Italy's official state art, but failed to do so. Mussolini was personally uninterested in art and chose to give patronage to numerous styles and movements in order to keep artists loyal to the regime. Opening the exhibition of art by the *Novecento Italiano* group in 1923, Mussolini said, "I declare that it is far from my idea to encourage anything like a state art. Art belongs to the domain of the individual. The state has only one duty: not to undermine art, to provide humane conditions for artists, to encourage them from the artistic and national point of view." Mussolini's mistress, Margherita Sarfatti, who was as able a cultural entrepreneur as Marinetti, successfully promoted the rival Novecento Group, and even persuaded Marinetti to sit on its board.

Although, in the early years of Italian Fascism, modern art was tolerated and even embraced, towards the end of the 1930s, right-wing Fascists took over the concept of "degenerate art" from Germany and condemned Futurism. In 1938, when he learned that Hitler wanted to include Futurism in a traveling exhibition of "degenerate art," Marinetti persuaded Mussolini to refuse to let it enter Italy.

*

Marinetti moved from Milan to Rome to be near the center of where things were happening. He became an academic despite his condemnation of academies, proclaiming "It is important that Futurism be represented in the Academy."

He married despite his condemnation of marriage, promoted religious art after the *Lateran Treaty* of 1929, and even reconciled himself with the Catholic Church, declaring that "Jesus was a Futurist."

*

There were other contradictions in his character: despite his nationalism, he was an international figure, educated in Egypt and in France, writing his first poems in French, publishing the Futurist Manifesto in a French newspaper, and tirelessly traveling to promote his movement.

Marinetti volunteered for active service in the Second World War, even though he was in his sixties. He died in Bellagio, Italy, in 1944, before the end of World War II.

Francis Picabia (1879-1953)

Francis Picabia (born François Marie Martinez Picabia (1879-1953) was a well-known painter and poet born of a French mother and a Spanish-Cuban father who was an attaché at the Cuban legation in Paris, France. His father was of aristocratic Spanish descent.

Born in Paris and financially independent, he studied under Fernand Cormon at the École des Arts Decoratifs in the late 1890s. In 1894, Picabia financed his stamp collection by copying a collection of Spanish paintings that belonged to his father. Switching the originals for the copies, without his father's knowledge, he then sold the originals.

*

Fernand Cormon took him into his academy at 104 Boulevard de Clichy in Paris - a nursery of young talent where Van Gogh and Toulouse-Lautrec had previously studied. From the age of 20, Picabia lived of his paintings, before inheriting money from his mother.

In the beginning of his own career, from 1903 to 1908, Picabia was influenced by the impressionist paintings of Alfred Sisley, as his favorite subjects had become churches, lanes, roofs of Paris, riverbanks, washhouses, lanes and barges.

When people questioned his sincerity by objecting to his copies of Sisley, or that his cathedrals looked like Monet, it didn't bother him. He sold well: *Bords de l'Yonne, effet du matin* for 1220 francs, a record price at the time.

In 1909, Picabia married Gabrielle Buffet, and that same year he came under the influence of the cubists and the Golden Section (Section d'Or). Later, around

1911, he joined the *Puteaux Group*, which met at the studio of Jacques Villon in the village of Puteaux. There he became friends with artist Marcel Duchamp and close friends with Guillaume Apollinaire. Other group members included Albert Gleizes, Roger de La Fresnaye, Fernand Léger and Jean Metzinger.

In 1913, Picabia was the only member of the Cubist group to personally attend the New York Armory Show, and Alfred Stieglitz gave him a solo exhibition at his gallery *291*. The magazine *291* devoted an entire issue to him. In New York, Picabia also met Man Ray for the first time.

*

His wife, Gabrielle Buffet, was the highly intelligent and lively daughter of a French senator. At the end of 1916 the couple had left the wartime discomforts of Paris and came to Spain on a special government mission.

In Barcelona, within a small circle of refugee artists that included Marie Laurencin and Robert and Sonia Delaunay, he started his well-known *Dada Periodical 391*, modeled on Stieglitz's own magazine. The subject matter of *391* was mainly literary and full of aggression against everybody and everything.

At the occasion of an exhibition at the Galerie Wolfsberg, in September 1918, Piccabia came to Zurich. In a group exhibition, together with Arp, Janco, Richter and others, Picabia exhibited a series of pictorially almost disembodied "machine pictures." These pictures incorporated words and names designed to carry the subject matter of the picture outside the frame. "Here obviously, was a true *painter*, but he hardly *painted* at all", remembers Hans Richter. (Richter, p. 71)

"Viewed in retrospect, Picabia's arrival marks the end of an era in the history of Zurich Dada...Picabia's first appearance, plying us all with champagne and whisky in the Elite Hotel, impressed us in every possible way. He had wit, wealth, poetry and a Goya head set directly on his shoulders with no intervening neck; he was a cynic and had the vitality of an Andalusian bull. A globetrotter in the middle of a global war! ...He had inexhaustible powers of invention, he was rich, and he was independent, materially and mentally, intellectually and creatively. An artistic temperament which demanded spontaneous self-expression was matched in him with an intellect that could no longer see a meaning in this world at all." (Richter, pp.71-72)

And indeed: In Zurich, the proverbial bad weather may have contributed to the fact that Picabia had to seek treatment for depression and suicidal impulses.

Back in Barcelona, where Picabia had traveled under the rather short-lived pretext of making purchases for some French military department, he had made himself a suspect by his failure to purchase anything.

Under these circumstances, his departure for New York appears to have been an obvious step. When Picabia arrived in New York, Duchamp was already there. So was Man Ray, a famous name from Philadelphia.

With the help of Duchamp, he then continued his *391* periodical in the United States.

For the farewell to Dada at the "Bauhausfest" in Weimar, in May 1922, Picabia was prudently absent, having completely withdrawn from the movement.

In 1924, together with Duchamp and Dermée, he founded the *Instantaneis* movement, sometimes called the last offshoot of Dada. The word "Instananeism" emphasized yet again the central experience of Dada as Picabia saw it: the spur of the instant.

That same year he appeared in the René Clair surrealist film *Entr'acte*, firing a cannon from a rooftop. The film served as an intermission piece for Picabia's avant-garde ballet *Relâche* (Relax), which premiered at the *Théâtre des Champs-Elysées*, with music by Erik Satie.

In 1925, Picabia returned to figurative painting and during the 1930s became a close friend of Gertrude Stein. In the early 1940s he moved to the south of France, where his work took a surprising turn, as he produced a series of paintings based on the nude glamour photos in French "Girlie" magazines like *Paris Sex-Appeal*. Some of these works went to an Algerian merchant who sold them on, which is how Picabia came to decorate brothels across North Africa under the Occupation during World War II.

Before the end of the War, Picabia returned to Paris where he resumed abstract painting and writing poetry. In the spring of 1949, a large retrospective of his work was held at the Galerie René Drouin in Paris.

Francis Picabia died in Paris in 1953 and was interred in the *Cimetière de Montmartre*. In 2003, a single Picabia painting once owned by André Breton sold for $1.6 million.

Pablo Picasso (1881-1973)

Picasso, whose lifespan included the periods of Cubism, Dadaism and Surrealism, is too big a name to be skipped here. Yet, so much has been written about his work and life as a painter and lover that I shall limit the subject in this book to no more than a few sketchy remarks.

Picasso was still born. Had it not been for the presence of his uncle, Dr. Salvador Ruiz, who saved his life by exhaling cigar smoke into his nostrils, young Pablo would never have lived.

If the length of all the given names is any indication of how many expectations were placed from the very beginning in young Pablo Picasso, then the pressure on him from early childhood on must have been extreme.

Indeed, Picasso was baptized as *Pablo Diego José Francisco de Paula Juan Nepomuceno María de los Remedios Cipriano de la Santísima Trinidad Ruiz y Picasso*. His father, Ruiz, was an art teacher and a painter, specializing in naturalistic depictions of birds and other game. His ancestors were minor Spanish aristocrats.

With so many names of saints and proof of family provenance upon his shoulders, it is not surprising that he showed a passion and a skill for drawing from an early age. According to his mother, young Pablo's first words were "piz, piz", a shortening of lápiz (Spanish word for pencil). From the age of seven, Picasso received formal artistic training from his father in figure drawing and oil painting. Ruiz was a traditional, academic artist and instructor who believed that proper training required disciplined copying of the masters and drawing the human body from plaster casts and live models.

119

When Pablo was 13 and studying at the School of Fine Arts in Barcelona, his father rented a small room close to the family home for him, so the son could work alone. Yet Ruiz checked up on his son numerous times every day, making sure young Pablo was not getting diverted from what the father wanted him to become.

It worked! Today, Picasso is best known for co-founding the Cubist movement and for the wide variety of styles embodied in his work. Among his most famous paintings are the proto-Cubist work *Les Demoiselles d'Avignon* (1907), the abstract image of his lady friends in a brothel at the Calle Avignon in Barcelona, and *Guernica* (1937), which depicts the German bombing of Guernica during the Spanish Civil War.

*

During his years in Paris, many of them as a communist activist, Picasso entertained a distinguished crowd of friends on the Montmartre hill and at the Montparnasse quarter, which included André Breton, Guillaume Apollinaire, writer Alfred Jarry, and Gertrude Stein.

Picasso was befriended with most of the great names of the Dadaist and Surrealist movements, but never agreed to join any group, thus creating and maintaining his special image of being bigger than life.

Pablo Picasso died on 8 April 1973 in Mougins, France, while entertaining friends for dinner. His final words were: "Drink to me, drink to my health, you know I can't drink any more." He was interred at the Chateau of Vauvenargues near Aix-en-Provence, a property he had acquired back in 1958.

Man Ray (1890-1976)

Man Ray, born Emmanuel Radnitzky, was a big name in the Dada and pre-Dada era. Born in Philadelphia to Russian-Jewish immigrants, he was an American artist who spent most of his career in Paris, France.

Probably best described as a modernist, he was a significant contributor to both the Dada and Surrealist movements, although his ties to each of them were informal.

Man Ray's basic tool was the camera. Best known in the art world for his avant-garde photography, he also invented the *Rayograph,* whereby an object on photographic paper was briefly exposed to light. Richter describes this discovery as a "Gordian stroke: photography without a camera. By placing objects on a piece of photographic paper and lighting them from a particular angle, he created new poetic vistas. He called them Rayograms." **(Richter, p. 98)**

Man Ray produced major works in a variety of media, but considered himself a painter above all. His early paintings display elements of cubism. Upon befriending Marcel Duchamp, who was interested in showing movement in static paintings, Man Ray's works also begun to depict movement of the figures, such as in the repetitive positions of the skirts of the dancer in *The Rope Dancer Accompanies Herself with Shadows.*

In 1915, Man Ray had his first solo show of paintings and drawings. His first proto-Dada object, an assemblage entitled *Self-Portrait*, was exhibited the following year. He produced his first significant photographs in 1918.

Abandoning conventional painting, Man Ray involved himself with Dada. *Enigma of Isidore Ducasse* is an unseen object (a sewing machine) wrapped in cloth and tied up with a cord. Another work from this period, *Aerograph* (1919), was done with airbrush on glass.

In 1920, Man Ray helped Duchamp make his first machine and one of the earliest examples of kinetic art, *The Rotary Glass Plates*, composed of glass plates turned by a motor. That same year Man Ray, Katherine Dreier and Duchamp founded the Societé Anonyme, an art collection which in effect was the first museum of modern art in the U.S.

Hans Richter remembers: "Man Ray began his career as a painter, and from the very start he was a publicity expert with all the tricks of the trade at his fingertips and oil paint behind his ears. Following the example of Alfred Stieglitz, he became a photographer as well as a painter.

"The first work of his I saw was called *Boardwalk* and was the trademark of the New York Dada group. It was a chessboard, which he had made into a work of art by adding anti-artistic knobs and bits of rope...

"Despite all the humor that is apparent in his works, his composed and well-groomed exterior bears, by preference, a distinctly melancholy air – which he can shake off as soon as a pretty woman comes within reach. His ideas on life tend towards pessimism...

"He has the attitude to life of one who waits rather than one who expects. His skepticism with regard to humanity is boundless. This he had in common with Marcel Duchamp. They became close friends,...two chess-players in perfect harmony." (Richter pp. 96-97)

Man Ray died in Paris in 1976 and is buried in Montparnasse. His widow, Juliet, summed up the artist's life in the epitaph inscribed on his tombstone: "Unconcerned, but not indifferent."

Hans Richter (1888-1976)

Hans Richter was born into a prominent Jewish family in Berlin. There, he commenced his art training at the Academy of Art, before continuing his studies at the *Académie Julian* in Paris. Developing an avant-garde style, Richter was strongly influenced by artists he met at Berlin's *Sturm Gallery*, as well as the expressionistic work of *Die Brücke* and the *Blaue Reiter* groups. His deeply colored early paintings - portraits, landscapes, and urban scenes such as *Workers (*1912) and *Flute Player* (1905) - depict dramatic and mysterious themes, thus reflecting his contact with German Expressionism and Cubism.

*

During World War I, after being drafted into the German army, Richter was wounded and discharged. Here is Hans Richter in his own words:

"I myself came to Zurich through a curious accident. In September 1914, shortly after the outbreak of war, when I already had my mobilization papers for the German army in my pocket, some friends threw a farewell party. Among them were the two poets Ferdinand Hardekopf and Albert Ehrenstein. There was no knowing how, where and when we might meet again, and so, to cheer me up, Ehrenstein made this suggestion: 'If the three of us are still alive, let us meet at the *Café de la Terrasse* in Zurich in exactly two years from now, on September 15th, 1916, at three in the afternoon.' I knew neither Zurich nor the Café de la Terrasse, and my hopes of being there seemed more than slender.

"After eighteen month's war service, I was discharged, hobbling on two sticks, and suddenly remembered that improbable rendezvous. I was to have my first comprehensive exhibition at the Hans Goltz gallery in Munich in July 1916, so I should be more or less half way to Zurich, and as I had just married the nurse who had looked after me at the military hospital, we decided to go to Zurich, via Munich, for our honeymoon. In the middle of a war this was rather a forlorn hope, but with much patience and ingenuity, and a pile of recommendations, we arranged it. On September 15th at three o'clock in the afternoon, I was in the Café de la Terrasse - and there, waiting for me, sat Ferdinand Hardekopf and Albert Ehrenstein. This unlikely encounter, like something in a dream, was followed by another. A few tables away sat three young men. When Ehrenstein, Hardekopf and I had exchanged our news, they introduced me to the three young men: Tristan Tzara, Marcel Janco and his brother Georges. So it was that I landed on both feet, squarely inside what was already called the Dada group...In the next few days I was taken to meet the other members of the group - Emmy Hennings I already knew from the old Café des Westens in Berlin. And so I became a member of the family and remained one until peace came and Dada Zurich ended." (Richter, pp.27-28)

*

Works from this period include woodcuts, Dada head, and abstracted portraits of his friends and associates, such as his visionary 1917 Portrait of Emmy Hennings. Consistent with his collaboration with Dada,

Richter's art from 1916-1919 is particularly inspired by the relationship between music and visual expression.

"Richter met Ferruccio Busoni, who encouraged him to apply the principles of musical counterpoint to pictorial art. He remembers that *something musical*, a *melody of forms and colors*, had always haunted him."
(Richter – Postscript by Werner Haftmann , p. 220)

That same year, a happy chance brought him together with Viking Eggeling, who was already working on the same problem. Richter describes this encounter as follows:

"One day, early in 1918, Tzara knocked on the thin partition between our rooms in the Hotel Limmatquai in Zurich, and asked me to come and meet the Swedish painter Viking Eggeling. He had mentioned this artist several times before, and had hinted that he was experimenting with similar ends in view. I found a burly man of average height, with an aquiline nose and the brilliant blue eyes of a Viking. Eggeling showed me a drawing. It was as if someone had laid the sibylline books open before me. I *understood* at once what it was all about. Here, in its highest perfection, was a level of visual organization comparable with counterpoint in music: a kind of controlled freedom or emancipated discipline, a system within which chance could be given a comprehensible meaning. This was exactly what I was now ready for." **(Richter, p.62)**

"In 1919, Richter and Eggeling moved to an estate owned by Richter's parents at Klein-Koelzig, near Berlin, and worked in close corporation for three years.

"Their purpose was to make the picture become a rhythmical development of formal themes. In thousands of experiments, both artists attempted to build complicated rhythmic sequences out of simple elements. The technique they used to achieve - a temporal sequence of movements - had already been applied by Delauny. They elongated the picture so that it was impossible to take it in at one glance, thus forcing themselves, and the beholder, to read off the individual pictorial elements one after the other, as one reads a message written on a strip of paper. A study of Chinese calligraphy soon suggested a better solution - the scroll. As this unrolled, the formal theme was developed in a period of time comparable with that required for the unfolding of a fugue in music. In 1919 Richter painted his first scroll picture." (Richter – Postscript, pp. 220-1)

*

Film-making was the logical next step. In 1921, Richter finished his first abstract films, *Rhythm 21,* followed by *Film Study* (1926), and *Ghosts Before Breakfast* (1927). Censored by the German government during the Nazi regime as "degenerate art," these films are now considered classics of early avant-garde cinema.

Richter's manipulation of film speeds, his experimentation with camera movements and rapidly spliced shots were revolutionary progressions in cinema and shocked and delighted his audiences.

*

Following the outbreak of World War II, Richter moved from Switzerland to the United States in 1940 and became an American citizen. He founded the *Film Institute of City College*, New York, where he remained a supervisor and professor for 14 years. During this time Richter directed 2 feature films, *Dreams That Money Can Buy* (1947) and *8x8: A chess Sonata* (1957), in collaboration with his old friends Max Ernst, Marcel

Duchamp, Fernand Leger, Alexander Calder, Man Ray, Jean Cocteau, Paul Bowles and others. The piece was partially filmed on the lawn of Richter's summer house in Southbury, Connecticut.

In 1957, he finished his *Dadascope* with original poems and prose spoken by their creators: Hans Arp, Marcel Duchamp, Richard Huelsenbeck, Raoul Hausmann, and Kurt Schwitters.

*

Early on in his career, Richter developed and propagated ideas on art based on what he called an *Universelle Sprache* (A universal language), free of national frontiers, and comprehensible to all people.

After 1958, Richter split his time between Ascona, Switzerland, and his house in Connecticut, and he returned to painting.

Hans Richter received several publicly recognized awards during his life, including the *International Prize for Film* in Venice (1947), and the *Art Prize of the City of Berlin* (1967). He had over 158 exhibitions, wrote more than 23 books, and produced, directed or wrote some 30 films.

Richter was a hard worker until, in 1976, he died at age 88, in Minusio, near Locarno, Switzerland.

Kurt Schwitters (1887-1948)

Kurt Schwitters was born on June 20, 1887, in Hanover, as the only child of Edward Schwitters and his wife Henriette. His parents owned a ladies' clothes shop, then sold the business in 1898 and used the money to buy five properties in Hanover, which they rented out, thus allowing the family to live off the income for the rest of Schwitter's life in Germany.

Schwitters married his cousin Helma Fischer on October 5, 1915. Their first son, Gerd, died within a week of birth. Their second, Ernst, was born on November 16, 1918, and was to remain close to his father for the rest of his life, up to and including a shared exile in London.

After studying art at the Dresden Academy alongside Otto Dix and George Grosz, (although Schwitters was unaware of their work), Schwitters returned to Hanover and started his artistic career as a post-impressionist. As the First World War progressed, his work became darker and gradually developed a distinctive expressionist tone. Expressionism was the predominantly German artistic movement, best exemplified by *Die Brücke* and by the paintings of Emil Nolde and Ernst Ludwig Kirchner in particular.

In 1918, Schwitters' art changed dramatically as a direct consequence of Germany's economic, political and military collapse at the end of the First World War. Schwitters came into contact with Herwarth Walden's gallery *Der Sturm*, where he showed two of his semi-abstract expressionist landscapes in June of 1918, which led directly to meetings with members of the Berlin Avant-garde, including Raoul Hausmann, Hannah Höch and Hans Arp in the autumn of 1918.

Raoul Hausmann recalls the meeting in his *Courrier Dada:* " 'My name is Schwitters, Kurt Schwitters.' I had never heard the name before. We sat down and I asked, 'What do you do?' 'I am a painter and I nail my pictures together.'"

But when he asked to join the *Club Dada*, he was rejected by Huelsenbeck because of his links to *Der Sturm* and to the Expressionists in general, which the Dadaists saw as hopelessly romantic.

"This first rebuff that Schwitters received in Berlin caused him to set up shop on his own in Hanover, under the name of *Merz*, which he extracted from the word 'Commerzbank'." (Richter, p. 138)

By the end of 1919, Schwitters had become famous, following his first one-man exhibition at *Der Sturm* and the publication of the poem *An Anna Blume* (For Anna Flower), a Dadaist non-sensical love poem.

His work was more in tune with the Zurich group's Dada performance and abstract art than with the Berlin Dada agitated political propaganda approach, and indeed, examples of his work were published in the last Zurich Dada publication, *der Zeltweg*, on November 1919, alongside the work of Hans Arp and Sophie Tauber.

"He got on especially well with Arp. In many ways they spoke the same language, a kind of sophisticated schizophrenic dialect, a German raised above all conventions. From this language they conjured colorful rhythms, associations and forms, and consequently new thoughts, new experiences and new sensations...

"Schwitters' art and his life were a living epic. Something dramatic was always happening. The Trojan war cannot have been as full of incidents as one day in Schwitters' life. When he was not writing poetry, he was pasting up collages. When he was not pasting, he was building his column, washing his feet in the same water as his guinea-pigs, warming his paste-pot in the bed, feeding the tortoise in the rarely-used bathtub, declaiming, drawing, printing, cutting up magazines, entertaining his friends, publishing *Merz,* writing letters, loving, designing all Guenther Wagner's printing and publicity material (for a regular fee), teaching academic drawing, painting really terrible portraits, which he loved, and which he then cut up and used piecemeal in abstract collages, assembling bits of broken furniture into *Merz* pictures, shouting to Helmchen, his wife, to attend to Lehmann, his son, inviting his friends to very frugal luncheons...and in the midst of all this he never forgot, wherever he went, to pick up discarded rubbish and stow it in his pockets. All this he did with an instinctive alertness of spirit, an intensity that never failed." (Richter, pp. 138-139)

Schwitters was to use the term *Merz* for the rest of his career. While these works were usually collages incorporating found objects, including bus tickets, old wire and fragments of newsprint, *Merz* also included artist's periodicals, sculptures, sound poems and what would later be called *installations*.

Thanks to Schwitters' lifelong patron and friend Katherine Dreier, his work was exhibited regularly in the US from 1920 onwards. In the late 1920s he became a well-known typographer for the City of Hannover. Many of his designs, test prints and proof sheets appeared in *Merz*. In a manner similar to the typographic experimentation by Herbert Bayer at the *Bauhaus*, and Jan Tschichold's "Die neue Typographie," Schwitters experimented with the creation of a new, more phonetic, alphabet in 1927. Some of his types were cast and used in his work.

Schwitters composed and performed an early example of sound poetry, his *Ursonate* (Original Sonata or Primeval Sonata - 1922-32). The poem was inspired by Raoul Hausmann's poem *fmsbw*, which Schwitters had heard recited by Hausmann in Prague, in 1921. Schwitters performed the piece regularly, developing and extending it, until finally publishing his notations for the recital in the last Merz periodical in 1932.

Alongside his collages, Schwitters also dramatically altered the interiors of a number of spaces throughout his life. The most famous was his *Merzbau*, the transformation of six rooms of the family house in Hanover. This first such project took place very gradually: works started around 1923, but the first room was not finished until 1933. Schwitters subsequently extended the *Merzbau* to other areas of the house until he fled to Norway in early 1937.

Early photos show Schwitters *Merzbau* with a grotto-like surface and various columns and sculptures, possibly referring to similar pieces by Dadaists, including the Great Plasto-Dio-Dada-Drama by Johannes Baader, shown at the *First International Dada Fair* in Berlin, 1920. Work by Raoul Hausmann and Sophie Tauber, among others, were incorporated. Photos of the *Merzbau* were exhibited at the MoMA in New York in 1936.

The political situation in Germany under the Nazi regime continued to deteriorate throughout the 1930s. Schwitters lost his typographical contract with the City of Hanover in 1934, and examples of his work in German museums were confiscated and publicly ridiculed in 1935. When his close friends Christof and Luise Spengemann and their son Walter were arrested by the Gestapo in August 1936, the situation had clearly become perilous.

On January 2, 1937, Schwitters was wanted for an "interview" with the Gestapo. He fled Hanover to join his son Ernst in Norway, who had already left Germany a few days earlier. Schwitters' wife Helma decided to remain in Hanover to manage their four properties. That same year, his *Merz* pictures were included in the Nazi exhibition *Entartete Kunst* in Munich, making his return impossible. Helma visited her husband in Norway for a few months every year, until the outbreak of the Second World War. The joint celebrations for his mother Henriette's 80th birthday and his son Ernst's engagement held in Oslo on June 2, 1939, was the last time the couple would meet.

When the Nazis invaded Norway in 1940, Schwitters fled to England, where he was interned for a short period on the Lofoten Islands. From June 8th to 18th, 1940, Schwitters fled to Scotland with his son on the icebreaker Fridtjof Nansen.

Branded by now as an enemy alien, he was moved between various internment camps in Scotland and England, until he finally ended up in Douglas Camp, Isle of Man, where he spent a year and a half.

After an intervention from Alexander Dorner of the Rhode Island School of Design, Schwitters was finally released on November 21, 1941.

His wife Helma died of cancer on October 29, 1944, and Schwitters only heard of her death in December. About the same time, he discovered that his *Merzbau* in Hanover had been destroyed during an allied air raid.

On June 27, 1945, after his son returned to Norway, Schwitters left London for the Lake District with his new companion, Edith Thomas, (known as "Wantee" for her habit of always asking guests if they'd like a cup of tea).

In August, 1947, he began the work on his last *Merzbau* in Elterwater, near Ambleside, which he called the *Merzbarn*. This enterprise was made possible by a grant from the *MoMA* New York, a grant that had originally been intended to help restore the Hanover original. One wall of the *Merzbarn* is now exhibited at the Hatton Gallery in Newcastle, while the shell of the barn remains in Elterwater.

Plagued by health problems in his remaining years, including temporary blindness in 1946 and numerous strokes, Schwitters died in Kendal, England, on January 8th, 1948, of a heart attack, and was buried in Ambleside. His grave was unmarked until 1966, when a stone was erected with the inscription *Kurt Schwitters - Creator of Merz*. The stone remains as a memorial even though his body was later disinterred and reburied in Hanover.

Hans Richter nourished remorse as to the Dada group's lack of assistance towards their friend Kurt Schwitters after the War: "Instead of being grateful for all the shared memories, we allowed him, a German painter and poet, to die unrecognized in poverty and exile, and protected only by an English girl, Edith Thomas, and an English farmer by the name of Pierce. This does not perhaps strictly belong here, but I want to see Schwitters, and his work, in the perspective in which history will see him."(Richter,p.138)

Indeed, Kurt Schwitters is generally recognized today as the twentieth century's greatest master of collage.

Tristan Tzara (1896-1963)

Tristan Tzara (born Samuel or Samy Rosenstock, also known as S. Samyro) was a Romanian and French avant-garde poet, essayist and performance artist. He was also active as a journalist, a playwright, a literary and art critic, and a composer and film director.

Tzara was born in Moineşti, Bacău County, in the historical region of Moldavia. His parents were Romanian Jews who spoke Yiddish as their first language; both his father and grandfather were entrepreneurs in the forestry business. Tzara's mother was Emilia Rosenstock. Owing to the Romanian Kingdom's discrimination laws, the Rosenstocks were deemed "not emancipated," and thus Tzara only became a full citizen of the country after 1918.

Early on, the adolescent Tzara became interested in symbolism and co-founded the magazine *Simbolul,* together with Ion Vinea (with whom he also wrote experimental poetry) and painter Marcel Janco.

In 1914, Tzara had enrolled at the University of Bucharest, studying Mathematics and Philosophy, but did not graduate. During World War I, after briefly collaborating on Vinea's *Chemarea*, Tzara travelled to Zurich / Switzerland to join his friend Janco.

Tzara, shared his lodging with Marcel Janco, who was a student at the *Technische Hochschule*. After settling in Switzerland, the young poet almost completely discarded Romanian as his language of expression, writing most of his subsequent works in French.

In Zurich, the Romanian group met with the German anarchist and poet Hugo Ball and his young wife Emmy Hennings, a music hall performer. Hugo Ball recorded this period, noting that Tzara and Marcel Janco, like Hans Arp, Arthur Segal, Otto van Rees, Max

Oppenheimer, and Marcel Słodki, "readily agreed to take part in the cabaret."

Tzara's shows at the Cabaret Voltaire and Zunfthaus zur Waag, as well as his poetry and art manifestos, became a main feature of early Dadaism. Tzara's work represented Dada's nihilistic side, in contrast with the more moderate approach favored by Hugo Ball. In Tzara's words: "The beginning of Dada were not the beginning of art, but of disgust."

(Rubin, William S. - Dada, Surrealism, and their Heritage, MoMA, 1967)

The shows that Tzara staged in Zurich often turned into scandals or riots, and he was in permanent conflict with the Swiss law enforcers.

Tzara was the ideal promoter of Dada, and his position as a modern poet enabled him to make contact with contemporary poets and writers in other countries, particularly in France and Italy. Marinetti, the founder and spokesman for the Italian Futurist movement, exchanged letters with Tzara, and his Futurist Manifesto influenced the Zurich Dada movement profoundly.

Tzara created a list of so-called "Dada presidents," who represented various regions of Europe. It included not only names like Aragon, Arp, Breton, Ernst and Fraenkel, but also writers and composers like Johannes Baader, Julius Evola, Vicente Huidobro, Maja Kruscek, Rafael Lasso de la Vega, Francesco Meriano and Igor Stravinsky.

While active as a promoter, Tzara also published his first volume of collected poetry, the 1918 *Vingt-cinq poèmes* (Twenty-five Poems).

A major event took place in the autumn of 1918, when Francis Picabia, who was then publisher of the *391* magazine and a distant Dada affiliate, visited Zurich and introduced his colleagues there to his nihilistic views on art and reason.

Richter credited Picabia's Zurich visit with boosting the Romanian author's status, but also with making Tzara himself "switch suddenly from a position of balance between art and anti-art into the stratospheric regions of pure and joyful nothingness." (Richter pp.70-71)

The movement subsequently organized its last major Swiss show, held at the *Saal zur Kaufleuten*, with choreography by Susanne Perrottet, Sophie Taeuber-Arp, and with the participation of Käthe Wulff, Hans Heusser, Tzara, Richter and Walter Serner. It was there that Serner read from his 1918 essay, whose very title advocated *Letzte Lockerung* (Last Letting Loose): this part is believed to have caused the subsequent mêlée, during which the public attacked the performers and succeeded in interrupting, but not cancelling, the show.

*

In 1919, after World War I came to an end, Tzara made his entrance as *Monsieur Dada* in Paris. Richter remembers: "He arrived one evening from the Gare de l'Est (Eastern Railroad Station), carrying a little suitcase, and rang Picabia's doorbell. The startled Picabia, who had invited him but was not expecting him, put him up for the night on their sofa." (Richter, p. 168)

Despite his unimpressive entry into Paris, Tzara soon became the focus of attention in avant-garde circles. The group of young poets, Breton, Aragon, Soupault and others, were awaiting him, and so he joined the staff of *Littérature* magazine.

Defending his principles against André Breton and Francis Picabia, Tzara soon became involved in some major polemics, which led to Dada's split. According to Richter, tensions between Breton and Tzara had surfaced in 1920, when Breton first made known his wish to do away with musical performance altogether and alleged that Tzara was merely being repetitive.

The *Gas Heart* or *The Gas-Operated Heart* (Le Cœur à gaz) was first staged in Paris, as part of the 1921 *Dada Salon* at the Galerie Montaigne. It was written as a parody of classical drama in three acts, despite being short enough to qualify as a one-act play. A part-musical performance that featured ballet numbers, it was one of the most recognizable plays inspired by the anti-establishment trend known as Dadaism. Tzara's notes for ending the piece read as follows:

"This is how the play is printed to end. But, in the spirit of Dada, it works better if it is staged with no end. The actors should just continue indefinitely *ad lib,* either repeating old lines or improvising new ones, until the audience either leaves the theatre or literally forces an end, perhaps by physical violence. The point of the play is to trick the audience into becoming part of the performance, even better if against their will."
(Tzara, Tristan – The gas heat: the Dada anti-masterpiece of drama – translation by Eric v. d. Luft – Gegensatz Press, N. Syracuse, New York, 2008)

By that time, the Dada shows were such common occurrences that audiences expected to be insulted by the performers. But a more serious crisis occurred in May, when Dada organized the *Mock trial of Maurice Barrès*, whose early affiliation with the Symbolists had been shadowed by his reactionary stance. "Barrès had been the ideal of many of the Dadaists in their youth. He had then turned *traitor* and become the mouthpiece of the reactionary newspaper *L'Éco de Paris.*" (Richter p. 184)

In that mock trial, Georges Ribemont-Dessaignes was the prosecutor, Aragon and Soupault the defense attorneys, with Tzara, Ungaretti, Benjamin Péret and others posting as witnesses (a mannequin stood in for Barrès). Péret upset Picabia and Tzara by refusing to make the trial an absurd event, and by introducing a political subtext with which Breton finally agreed.

"After the Barrès affair the paths of the three groups led respectively by Breton, Tzara and Picabia began to diverge...However, there was yet no breach between the different groups despite the open disagreements about the Barrès 'trial'. In the summer of 1921 we find Breton and Tzara with Ernst and Arp at Imst in Tirol, where they published one more Dada document together: *Dada in the Open Air*. Exhibitions of the work of Man Ray, who had just turned up in Paris, and Picabia should also be mentioned. But the element that had held the Dada movement together, the fury of public opinion, had lost some of its cohesive power, and not only through the 'trial' of Barrès. Not much remained of the explosive shock of arousal, the anti, which had been Dada's original moral credo." (Richter, pp. 184-186)

Breton openly attacked Tzara in a February 1922 article of *Le Journal du Peuple*, where the Romanian writer was denounced as "an impostor," avid for publicity. In March, Breton initiated the *Congress for the Determination and Defense of the Modern Spirit* and used the occasion to strike out Tzara's name from among the Dadaists, citing in his support Dada's Huelsenbeck, Serner, and Christian Schad. Backing up his statement by a note supposedly authored by Huelsenbeck, Breton also accused Tzara of opportunism, claiming that he had planned wartime editions of Dada works in such a manner as not to upset actors on the political stage, making sure that German Dadaists were not made available to the public in countries subject to the *Supreme War Council*'s control.

Tzara, who reportedly attended the Congress only as a means to subvert it, responded to the accusations that same month, arguing that Huelsenbeck's note was fabricated and that Schad had not been one of the original Dadaists. Much later, rumors reported by American writer and painter Brion Gysin (1916-1986) had it that Breton's claims also depicted Tzara as an informer for the *Prefecture* of Police.

In May 1922, Dada staged its own funeral. According to Hans Richter, the main part of this took place in Weimar, where the Dadaists attended a festival of the Bauhaus art school, during which Tzara proclaimed the elusive nature of his art:

DADA is a virgin microbe
DADA is against the high cost of living
DADA
limited company for the exploitation of ideas
DADA has 391 different attitudes and colors according to the sex of the president
It changes - affirms - says the opposite at the same time - no importance - shouts - goes fishing.
Dada is the chameleon of rapid and self-interested change.
Dada is against the future. Dada is dead. Dada is absurd. Long live Dada. Dada is not a literary school, howl
(dada manifesto on feeble love and bitter love by tristan tzara)

After July 1922, Marcel Janco, who had returned to Romania, rallied with Vinea in editing Contimporanul, which published some of Tzara's earliest poems, but never offered space to any Dadaist manifesto.
Reportedly, the conflict between Tzara and Janco had a personal note: Janco later mentioned "some dramatic quarrels" between his colleague and him. They avoided each other for the rest of their lives and Tzara even struck out the dedications to Janco from his early poems.

*

Breton places the end of Dada in 1924, when he issued the first *Surrealist Manifesto,* and Richter suggests, "Surrealism devoured and digested Dada."
(Richter, p. 194)

Tzara distanced himself from the new surrealist trend, disagreeing with its methods and, increasingly, with its politics. In 1923, he and a few other former Dadaists collaborated with Richter and the Constructivist artist El Lissitzky on the magazine *G.*

Tzara continued to write and became more seriously interested in the theater. In 1924, he published and staged the play *Handkerchief of Clouds*, which was soon included in the repertoire of Serge Diaghilev's *Ballet Russe*. He also collected his earlier Dada texts as *Seven Dada Manifestos,* which Marxist thinker Henri Lefebvre reviewed enthusiastically and later became one of Tzara's friends.

In 1925, Tristan Tzara married Greta Knutson in Stockholm, with whom he had a son, Christophe (born 1927). A former student of painter André Lhote, Greta was known for her interest in phenomenology and abstract art. Around the same period, with funds from Knutson's inheritance, Tzara commissioned Austrian architect Adolf Loos, a former representative of the Vienna Secession whom he had met in Zurich, to build him a house in Paris. The rigidly functionalist *Maison Tristan Tzara*, built on Montmartre, was designed following Tzara's specific requirements and decorated with samples of African art.

In 1929, Tzara reconciled with Breton and sporadically attended the Surrealists' meetings in Paris. The same year, he issued the poetry book *De nos oiseaux* (About Our Birds).This period saw the publication of *The Approximate Man* (1931), alongside with the volumes *L'Arbre des voyageurs* (The Travelers'

Tree −1930), *Où boivent les loups* (Where The Wolves Drink -1932), *L'Antitête* (The Antihead -1933) and *Grains et issues* (1935). By then, it was also announced that Tzara had started work on a screenplay. In 1930, he directed and produced a cinematic version of *Le Cœur à barbe* (The Bearded Heart), starring Breton and other leading Surrealists.

Tzara became involved in further developing Surrealist techniques, and, together with Breton and Valentine Hugo, drew one of the better-known examples of E*xquisite Corpses*. At around the same time, Tzara's wife was also affiliated with the Surrealist group. However, her association ended when she parted with Tzara in the late 1930s.

In 1934, he joined France's Communist Party, of which he became a life-long member. He joined the Loyalists in the Spanish Civil War and later the French Resistance during World War II. He directed the cultural broadcast of the French Resistance in the south of France from 1943 to 1944, and also wrote for Resistance magazines. At the end of World War II he became a naturalized French citizen and also served a term in the French National Assembly.

Tzara died on December 24, 1963, in Paris.

PART III: ACTIVATE YOUR DADA-GENE!

Chapter 8

Dada Redefined

1. Discover your Dada-Gene

The highway of 20th century art is paved with negativities, and the American dream of wealth and happiness has been perverted by wars and depressions, by extreme pressure at the workplace, by unscrupulous marketing schemes, by unhealthy food habits, and by a never-ending stream of negative information.

At this day and age, as we are slipping away from a controlled environment with incremental changes into a renewed era of probable quantum leaps, it may be smart - or even imperative - to reassess our thought process. All indicators point to the fact that we are heading into a renewed era of prolonged pain. Yet, as always in periods of turmoil, one of the positive effects is that many windows of opportunity are opening up, opportunities to refresh our minds and to reflect upon the fundamental values of our lives.

One such beneficial side effect for the creative artist who lives in bad economic times is that there is now a window of opportunity to create original artistic works again.

More generally speaking, activating our Dada-Gene becomes a means for readjusting our value system. What we have come to accept as important economic achievements by creating "nest eggs" is becoming less relevant, as compared to the urge of expressing our inner dream world.

Dada becomes a new means to take time out, to reflect upon a deeper value system, and to express it in happy ways. We learn to accept the world "as is" in a Buddhist manner, while disregarding the ugly for the benefit of our inner peace and prospect of happiness.

It is true that the feeling of happiness is a state of well-being that cannot last for a prolonged period at a time. However, we can all thrive to achieve a permanent feeling of pleasure and satisfaction within ourselves. Such emotions lead us on the right track to enjoy a full expansion of our capabilities and to contribute to a better future for ourselves and our communities. And by doing so, life must not necessarily become dull, but may well include all kind of adventures and excitements.

And, yes, this means tolerance towards each other, tolerance for each of our personal life styles, since we all try to keep our individual identity in an environment of ever-increasing pressure to act like flocks of sheep.

Modern society is governed by two interacting extremes:

- The ever repetitive Commercial TV-spots that portray "how beautiful life could be, if only you swallowed Tylenol all day long," or "how much safer we would all feel if a single caretaker would manage all our many medical prescriptions;"
- And at the opposite end our permanent exposure to the ugly "breaking news" that get under our skin by drawing attention to the reality of so many repulsive wars, murders, political battles, drugs and deceptions, wherever we look around us.

The uninterrupted flow of negative news demonstrates how much we have become a culture of cynics, hopelessly addicted and indulging in ever more inventive forms of negativities.

The record of 20th century art is but a mirror image of a progressively sliding slope, which has pushed ugliness and dissonances to limits never before seen.

These are not new thoughts. Back in 1957, in his *Memoirs of a Dada Drummer,* Richard Huelsenbeck wrote:

"In a highly industrialized country like America, in which universal conformity is lauded as a sound desire of the people, abstract art has become an occupational therapy for the emotionally threatened. It is a part of the general relaxation program. ... Naturally art is not dead, but it needs a new effort at clarification of its principles in an age that is giving itself over to self-destruction with terrifying enthusiasm." (Hulsenbeck, p.179)

*

If these lines were true over fifty years ago, how much further have we come to push the limits on our path to self-destruction! Indeed, any gallery or museum visit, or just even listening to a so called "classical concert," will reveal how many countless dissonances have entered even what were meant to be the most enjoyable leisure moments of our busy lives.

All that negative hype, to which we are exposed multiple times every day, is piling up in our minds and breeds pessimistic feelings that make us perceive the world in less than constructive ways. When the glass is sixty percent full, we tend to see it as forty percent empty. Like a slow growing cancer, our own negative attitude will end up affecting our families, our co-workers and our friends.

Our mind is engulfing in a downspin and our negative outlook on life is becoming a self-fulfilling prophecy for what we are going to get out of it. Jumping from one negative thought to the next is like leaping from one slippery rock to the next across the river of happiness, and when we finally reach the other side and look back on our life, we see nothing but a bunch of slippery rocks...

With this in mind, it appears to be high time for us to rethink our condition and reverse the dangerous negative trends of hype and disharmony in almost every section of modern society.

One example of where such an about-face could take place is through positive preaching in our churches; and indeed we are seeing some revival in many (although mostly rural) places. But at a time and age of the Internet and of so many scientific achievements it is hard for many of us to believe in so much religious hearsay, even though its morals are perfectly laudable and bring out a set of most valuable positive guidelines for our lives in communities. The one problem rational individuals have with religious teachings is the self-righteous, unforgiving and dogmatic attitude of many of our pastors and preachers.

Discovering our Dada-Gene may well be a solution. It is the approach to life with a positive mindset, comparable to the teachings of Buddha, in which religion as an institution is replaced by the concept of our belly button that symbolizes the (happy) center of our own world.

The aim is to become a sort of "human sundial," which only registers the sunny hours of our days in this life.

2. Dada: A Reverse Revolution?

Whenever the world was in turmoil, certain names came out from obscurity onto the stage of world history: Napoleon, Lenin, Hitler, Stalin and Mao. The same holds true for recurring themes, such as revolutions, socialism, capitalism, communism.

...and Dada in the Arts.

The history of the world is full of revolutions. Usually, when they are over and the cemeteries have been filled with dead bodies, things go back to normal, to square one, where it all started. And since we have little memory for pain, people don't learn from history.

Along with the changes of the political landscape, the art world underwent its own parallel revolutions: Cubism and Dadaism relating to World War I, Surrealism to World War II, and Abstract Expressionism (including Neo-Dadaism) reflecting the period of fear and depressed feelings throughout the Cold War between the United States and the Soviet Empire.

During the countless art movements of the 20th and 21st centuries, everything possible and imaginable has been tried and experimented, and nothing seems to be left that hasn't already been said, painted, or played. With Abstract Expressionism taking the idea of art to never before seen levels of disharmony, ugliness and despair, the question arises how much further the envelope could conceivably be pushed.

When an artist besmears a painting with dung, the culmination point of disgust has obviously been reached. Is there conceivably any phonier pretext to seek protection under the First Amendment? The problem is that lots of people apparently fall for it, thus opening the undeserved door of even a dialogue.

Now that the horrors of the world have extensively been expressed on canvas, in films and in the performing arts in the most gruesome ways, are we about to see a revolution from the revolution and go back to nature and the essentials of life? It seems that the only possible revolution left in an art world that prides itself of always being at the forefront of evolution, is what I would call a "Reverse Revolution."

But could there be such a notion as a "Reverse Revolution" in the arts? Throughout my life, I always believed that harmony, progress and revolution are not fundamentally conflicting notions.

Our culture is moving away from the sound of our voice to create calligraphy-like new symbolized languages through the Internet. By doing so, are we also in the process of moving away from the spoken word? Are we so much in a hurry, or have we become so disenchanted with the spoken word that we are about to give up on it?

*

The idea of the Dada-Gene is an attempt to take us back to the origin, just like the original Dada Movement of 1916 was trying to do in a child-like manner by breaking away from the news of the day and becoming nonsensical. The difference is that, hopefully this time, the newly tailored Dada dress will present itself in a positive and constructive way.

We have been distancing ourselves too far from nature. And the naïve approach of green-minded activists, who have never been to India or China to see *real* pollution, is barely a solution.

How about simply pitching a tent somewhere out there in a forest (as we do in our family) and listen to the bird songs in the crispy morning hours of a gorgeous upcoming day? If that were the message of the green activists, rather than living in the utopia of being able to change America's way of life, I would subscribe to it in a heartbeat.

Amidst the general malaise of our confused world, it is no wonder that many philosophical thoughts are now being borrowed from Buddhism and Taoism, in an attempt to revert back to a lifestyle of harmony with nature. It is an endeavor to look for beauty within the dreadful realities all around us, while accepting the world with all its negativities. It is also the desperate search for a mindset of harmony, which relates to my idea of a coming "Reverse Revolution."

3. A New Meaning for the Word Dada

Panta rei – everything flows. All is changing, all the time, including words and languages. While Shakespeare's vocabulary had only about 29,000 words, the current Oxford English dictionary contains roughly 171,000 words, with an additional 47,000 now listed as obsolete or only sparingly in use. And while the number of words has increased over the years, their meanings also evolved, got altered and rejuvenated.

One of those words is Dada. Back in 1916 the word Dada was loaded with negative connotations resulting from the dismays of the then raging First World War. The arts were blamed to be bourgeois institutions invented by bankers and industrialists, and the Dadaists were the revolutionaries who created an "anti-art" movement to destroy those museums as temples of the bourgeoisie.

And yet, even during those dark days of war, there was an obvious discrepancy between the revolutionary preaching, the personal lifestyle and the poetry writings of many Dadaists. Indeed, while the poems of the declared communists Hugo Ball and Tristan Tzara are of a non-compromising harshness in their form and substance, their less militant colleagues Hans Arp, George Grosz and Richard Huelsenbeck wrote poetry in which form and melody are full of classical harmony and rhymes, even though their content was mostly depressing.

Poetry has been described as that, which cannot be translated. Therefore, the English reader has to take my word that certain poems by Richard Huelsenbeck and George Grosz are entirely reminiscent of such classics as Friedrich Schiller and Johann Wolfgang von Goethe with respect to rigor in form, rhyme and sound, and only the content reveals a writer of the 20th century.

*

While familiarizing myself with the personal lives of the Dadaist, I was struck about the discrepancies between their public revolutionary preaching and their private lives, during which they often had lots of fun, went on excursions onto Switzerland's many hills and mountains, and generally enjoyed life away from the war zones raging in the other European countries.

The Dada movement was known as one of open revolt against the establishment, its outrage was meant for the outside world. "The Dadaist," said the German poet Richard Huelsenbeck "is a man of reality who loves wine, women and advertising." (Mark Harden's Artchive: "Dada and Surrealism")

No wonder then that Dada, from the beginning, has been many things. In *The Lecture on Dada*, published in the periodical *Merz* (Hannover 1924), Tristan Tzara wrote: "Dada is not at all modern. It is more in the nature of a return to an almost Buddhist religion of indifference. Dada covers things with an artificial gentleness, a snow of butterflies released from the head of a prestidigitator..."

And Kurt Schwitters wrote: "The word Merz had no meaning when I formed it. The meaning of the concept Merz changes with the change of the insight of those who continue to work with it."

In that same spirit, the word Dada has equally no other meaning than the one we decide to give it at any point in time, which - I strongly suggest - can and should be upgraded to become of a positive nature, a sort of remedy to fight an environment of cynicism and negativity that has been growing all around us like a malignant tumor for over fifty years.

4. Beauty and Harmony

Beauty and harmony may possibly best be defined by the negative: They are not what people experience all day long during regular working hours, nor what TV networks constantly run under the heading of "Breaking News." They are also not what eighty percent of the art galleries exhibit regularly in the "civilized world." They aren't either a part of those modern musical pieces that every concert hall of the world plays by smuggling in at every performance what they call "modern classical music," in order to educate the "ignorant public," for us to get "cultured" by listening to the cacophonies of a twelve-tone music.

No doubt: those artistic creations do reflect the "real world" in which we live. But the negative waves of our daily lives have become so overwhelming, that we don't need to be reminded of them in our moments of leisure, when we visit an art gallery or go to a concert. We are in dire need of beauty and harmony to surround us, to make our short appearance on the stage of life enjoyable and worthwhile.

*

Beauty involves the idea of being in balance with nature. In classical Greek, the word was related to "being of one's hour." A young woman in her natural state - like a ripe fruit - was considered beautiful. But a young woman trying to appear older, or an older woman trying to look younger, would not be seen as beautiful. People at a ripe old age, on the other hand, would be considered beautiful.

Another indicator of physical beauty relates to the idea of "averageness." A cousin of Charles Darwin, Sir Francis Galton, first noticed this in 1883 when he overlaid images of the faces of vegetarians and criminals to find out if there was a typical facial appearance of criminals. To his surprise, he realized that the composite images were always more attractive than the individual faces. In the 1980s, the American artist Nancy Burson (b.1948) combined the faces of three criminals. "I had expected a portrait of evil and ended up with the boy next door."
(Milner, Richard: *Darwin's Universe – Evolution from A to Z.* University of California Press, Ltd. London, England, 2009)

153

From an evolutionary standpoint, and in connection with the law of preservation of the species, it also appears logical that creatures find themselves particularly attracted to individuals of the opposite sex when those possess predominantly common, or average, features.

In that sense, beauty and harmony are really a standard of comparison, always relating to nature as our ultimate teacher. Early on, the Greek Pythagorean School became fascinated with what they called the **Golden Ratio**, a proportion, which appears to be particularly pleasing to the human eye. It says that, in a rectangle, the sum of the longer and the shorter side divided by the longer side should result in a constant factor (or close to same) as the longer side divided by the shorter side of that same rectangle. Mathematically, that constant factor results in **a ratio of 1.618.** For the practical artist it means that the longer side of his canvas should be 1.618 times longer than the short side, in order to be a perfect match to the Golden Rule.

*

Early on, when I began to paint interpretations of the old masters and Impressionist painters in the late 1970s, I became obsessed with the idea of harmony. I do believe that harmony is the most important element in nature and in art, including (paradoxically) the anti-art paintings of the Dadaists. Harmony is our inner raster that tells us artists (and the world that looks at our images) what is "right" and what is "wrong" in any given piece of art.

In the late 1980s I sent a post card of my large painting *The Last Judgment* to my friend and art dealer Max Bollag in Zurich. When I talked to him on the phone a few days later to ask him proudly what he thought of my painting he said: "I am sorry, my Dear, I have to tell you that this is not a great painting. Your sun is at the wrong place." These words bothered me to the point that it discouraged me from painting for quite a while, and I almost begun to hate this veteran of the arts.

But then, slowly, and over many years, I realized that Max had done me a great favor. I know now that the sun should be about ten inches to the right, and that my friend was entirely right. Max Bollag, with his rude comment, got me to realize that, no matter how traditional or avant-garde a painting may be, the harmony between space, lines, form and colors must always be "right."

*

Today, in my case, all of these considerations are not part of an intellectual evaluation for me any more when I do any of my drawings or paintings. They have become a part of me, a part of my guts so to speak, and I always make sure that everything is "right," even though that notion is so complex that it cannot be learned in any other way than empirically and only in very imperfect manners by the study of art. It is what traditionally is called "experience," or that which cannot be taught.

I believe it was Alberto Giacometti who once tried for the better part of a week to arrange an ashtray, a pencil, a ruler and an eraser on his desk in what he wanted to be "the ultimate, perfect and harmonious position," only to come to the conclusion that there is an almost infinite number of such positions at the beginning of his endeavor. But as he narrowed his choices down by joining one object after another, he realized that pretty soon his choices became limited and finally left him with no alternative: the placement of the last two objects had become mandatory.

*

In 1993, in collaboration with the robotics lab of the Electrical Engineering Department of Vanderbilt University in Nashville, I tried to find ways to program a robot to do harmonious drawings. Having a robot draw pictures is easy, but programming it to make them "beautiful" was - at the time - an almost impossible task. Today, I still believe that it can be done, and who knows where the future will take me, since I always follow my guts and never know what exciting new venture the next day may hold in store for me...

5. Creativity

The encyclopedia describes creativity as "*imaginative*" and contrary *to "boring."* I have often referred to boredom as the greatest plague of humanity. (I even go as far as to pretend that the history of the Crusades by European Christians against Muslims, back in the 11th century, was a means to go plunder entire cities and rape women in faraway countries, to escape boredom.)

I consider myself greatly creative; yet, a good dose of creativity can be every bit of a curse as the total lack thereof, at least from a monetary standpoint.

156

Creativity as a curse is the inability to stay on a single subject for an extended period of time for fear of becoming repetitive, whereas the road to financial success requires the exact opposite: staying obstinately the course on a single subject and repeating it almost indefinitely.

The most blatant example of creativity as a curse, versus repetitiveness as a financial blessing, is the history of Max and Dave Fleischer, the two brothers who, in their Hollywood studio, were the initial creators not only of virtually all of the well known animated Walt Disney characters (including Mickey Mouse, etc.), but also of Superman and many other icons of the animated world. Throughout their careers, the Fleischer Brothers were on the verge of bankruptcy, often forced to sell their creations, or had them stolen by countless copyright infringements. Walt Disney, on the other hand, known today as a great creative genius, was not very creative, but employed the creative minds to design his well-known characters, including even his own famous signature! His great financial success was derived from his obstinate pursuit of repetitiveness and being a perfectionist in every minute detail.

Can creativity be taught and learned? By surfing the Internet one is certainly encouraged to believe so. Indeed, in June of 2009, there were 13.1 million websites in English, French, Italian and Spanish that related to teaching creativity!

I discovered my own creativity while performing what I call my "gut paintings" and my "gut writings," without ever thinking about what I was doing next, nor even realizing that I was doing what the Surrealists had called "Automatic Drawings and Paintings" over eighty years ago. I was thoroughly thrilled to learn about my inner self and fascinated about my newly found sense of freedom.

But the minute I tried to intellectualize the process of creativity (as opposed to listening to my inner self) I succumbed to the danger of "cramping up" and guiding the creative process from my brain; and the resulting piece of art always reflected it in a negative way.

The problem of the beginner, who controls his or her creativity by the thought process of rendering memorized images, or thoughts, is the classical syndrome of the art student who is boxed into his scholarly knowledge. Therefore, when Picasso said "painting cannot be taught, but can only be found," or "the approach to artistic creation should be child-like," he definitely had a point.

In my case, 21 years of school education had to be eradicated, in order to brake through my level of consciousness. Early on, I found assistance in a half bottle of red wine before beginning my work. Then, after a few years, I didn't need the wine any more.

About "Producers" and "Consumers."

My premise is that the world is divided between producers and consumers. Ninety-five percent are consumers. They are the salary recipients, always depending on somebody else to make a living.

The producers are the entrepreneurs, the creators, the visual and performing artists, the composers, musicians, and the poets and writers. They all are compelled to create, to achieve, to imagine new ways of becoming ever better in whatever they do, to satisfy their sense of accomplishment, and to increase their well-being, while seeking what is commonly referred to as "happiness."

Whereas all producers are also consumers, the same cannot be said of the consumers. Their daily repetitive performance at the workplace inevitably invites them to continue the passive intake of other people's actions even after business hours, at home, or in the sports arena. They are the victims of the shallow soap operas, the constant TV marketing abuses, and of the perpetual "breaking (nonsensical) news."

*

It doesn't have to be that way. I pretend that all humans carry within them what I call the Dada-Gene, that powerful ability and tool to be creative and to enjoy the fantastic feeling of having accomplished something they can be proud of.

Now, let me tell you my personal story of how I discovered my own Dada-Gene:

Chapter 9

Dada-Gene: My Story

Riches versus Happiness

During my life I have met and known many of the world's rich and powerful men and women. Recently, as my family keeps growing, I lined them all up in my mind for a mental revue and asked myself whom we should adopt as a roll model for our own family. Incredibly, not a single name withstood that test. Upon closer exam, every single one of them had personal or family problems that wouldn't compensate for a status of fame and riches and result in "a happy family."

During that mental exercise, a famous German fairy tale came to my mind. It is the story of a young man who was sent out by his father to learn the trade of a miller and to look out for happiness in life. After years of hard work, his master declared him fit for life and gave him a large rock of solid gold as salary for his hard work during the past many years. On the young man's long way back to his parents, he met a man on a horse, and as he sweated and suffered under the heavy weight of his gold, he exchanged it against the man's horse. But a short while thereafter he got hungry, and when he met a man with a cow, he exchanged his horse against the cow, so he would always have milk to drink. But then again, he met a man with a goat and exchanged the cow against the goat, so he would get to his parent's home faster and still have milk to drink. Further along, he met a boy with a hen, and the idea of having eggs to eat and feathers to stuff his pillow with prompted him to exchange his goat for the hen. Finally, just as he saw his parents' house on the horizon, he met a lady with a basket full of eggs. Since those eggs would be able to produce many chicken, he exchanged his hen against the eggs. But then, shortly thereafter, he fell over a big root on his way and all the eggs fell on the ground and broke. Finally, he arrived happily at his parent's home. He had just lost his remuneration for many years of hard work through a chain of silly down-trades, but was glad to be home again.

The story was, of course, meant in a spirit of indoctrination to never gamble away one's fortune. Yet, recently I began to see it in a different light: that of the Buddha who values happiness above the worries of a large fortune that comes with so many strings attached.

My focus in life has recently shifted, as happiness has become my most important goal. This is why I am now often adding the letters BM (Beyond Money) to my signature.

*

Last night I had a dream. I was walking in a large crowd, and everybody around me was dressed in torn-up blue jeans and shabby T-shirts. Suddenly, a loud voice thundered from a loudspeaker and ordered everybody to go to City Hall to pick up a sticker. By order of the Government, the label had everybody's net worth printed and had to be prominently displayed by sticking it to all our foreheads, so we could easily be identified and categorized according to the right social order. "Too many people," said the speaker in a menacing voice, "are running around pretending to be rich, while - in fact - they are poor and don't belong into that privileged crowd." And then the voice continued: "And - on the other hand - when you are rich, the sticker helps the government to track you down and identify you by your sticker, so they can tax you according to your net worth."

"Thank God," I thought, "we are not there yet." And - upon a second thought - that cannot concern me, I have become B.M. since several years.

*

Two years ago, I got a fortune cookie at a Chinese restaurant, which I taped on the wall in front of me. It reads: "Do not follow where the path may lead. Go where there is no path...and leave a trail." It is the story of my life. A rugged path!

1. My Path to Dada

I was born into what is called a privileged family. During my adolescent years I never doubted that I was going to be a big time financial guru.

Paradoxically, since my early life, I also was a revolutionary. I read Karl Marx's *"Das Kapital"* when I was fourteen and studied the Russian language in Geneva with a lady in her eighties, who was introduced to me as one of Vladimir Lenin's former girlfriends, when the revolutionary champ was living in Switzerland, prior to the First World War. I had also subscribed to the Soviet party paper *ISVESTIA,* which was delivered to my home on a daily basis directly from Moscow. Yet, ironically, I was a hard core capitalist at heart, as I *knew* that one day I would be sitting on top of the world.

Then, in 1965, after a terrible train accident, I experienced a 32-minute cardiac arrest and was

163

subsequently hospitalized for a full year in Lausanne/Switzerland. Following my near-death experience, I spent several hours every day in the hospital wing of the terminally ill patients, in order to familiarize myself with the realities of death.

It was then that I intuitively began to see my future life as a Buddhist, a state of mind that I was going to cherish increasingly.

My path to becoming a Buddhist was, however, quite slow, since my mind was still set on the obsession of riches.

By 1976, I discovered my inner calling as an artist and, subconsciously, money became unimportant.

In 1982, at age 45, I left Europe with my wife and two sons to settle as an artist in Manhattan.

Anybody who was somebody in the New York art scene was young, had a graduate degree from Yale, or was teaching at Harvard, and had at least a 20-foot long résumé, full of awards, grants and museum exhibitions. All I had going for me was my resolve to become a good artist and a good writer. The odds were almost infinitely against me.

I did, however, bring a number of unique qualifications to the table: I had a profound knowledge of what good art is, and I had a vast life experience with countless worldwide travels under my belt. I was free of the legendary tunnel vision that characterizes so many other artists. In other words: I was going to challenge the system in spite of all the odds.

From an economic standpoint, things went from bad to worse by the year. I had long maintained that living in poverty was not necessary to produce good art. Now that I was there myself, I changed my opinion, and today I firmly believe that it is indeed essential to have gone through hardship in order to become a good artist.

The worst thing was that my visual memory is practically inexistent. Anybody will tell you that the number one qualification for an artist is to have a photographic memory, so he or she can paint a horse, a man, or a dog with great accuracy from memory. My brain doesn't work that way: While I have a thousand visions in my inner dream world, I was never able to capture nature artistically in any other form than with a camera.

Given that horrendous handicap, the only way for me to succeed was to draw or paint without any preconception, by bringing directly onto paper or canvas whatever the spur of the moment would inspire me to do. Unlike what any formal art education is ever teaching, I had to start with my brush on an empty canvas, not knowing the least bit of what the outcome was going to be. Then, after I had finished the first layer, I painted it over, and over, and over again, changing entirely the appearance of my canvas over many days, or months, until I finally had an acceptable painting in front of me.

And then there came an even larger problem, in that I was never satisfied with what I had done. How many times had I not finished a painting in the wee hours of the morning and tapped myself on my mental shoulder, being sure that I had just produced a masterpiece, only to wake up later that day and having to admit to myself that my beautiful painting was a piece of trash.

Today, though, I have reached a different level. I now believe that my lousy visual memory is my biggest asset. Since I am not burdened with haunting images from my museum - or gallery - visits that would make me a "copyist," I can easily vouch that each of my drawings and paintings is a unique and original work that emanates from my most inner dream world. I have produced over a thousand drawings and not two are identical, even though they all carry my rather unique style as a signature.

A few years ago, a painter friend told me while looking at my drawings that in her opinion I was a "Dadaist." I didn't give it much thought then.

*

Although I was forced from early childhood on to submit myself to a rigorous Christian-Protestant education regime, my interest in yoga and Buddhism goes back all the way to my pre-high school years. Already in my early teens I remember having uneasy feelings about organized religions.

Later, after traveling around the globe many times over, I had gained a pretty good understanding of the major world religions. And the more I saw and learned, the more tolerant I became towards the way other peoples of our planet pursue their search and relationship with an unseen higher authority somewhere out there, which seems to be an almost universal yearning of any culture throughout human history.

As for me, I have lived with a 5-foot Burmese temple Buddha since 1978. My Buddha reminds me on a daily basis of how to look at the big picture of life and how to straighten out my long-term priorities.

Sometime in 2007, it became clear to me that the long-term economic outlook was headed "for the tank." That it was time to take a deep breath and continue my Buddha-like attitude towards life. It was also the time when I discovered my Dada-Gene.

2. My Lifelong Dada Dream Drawings

Ever since I was a small boy I have been doing what people commonly call "doodling." As a kid, my school buddies were looking over my shoulder, and later in life - when I was attending one of those boring business or political conferences - my neighbors looked onto my paper sheet and lauded the "artistic qualities" of my drawings. None of them survived, but after my move to Manhattan I started to keep, and even exhibit some in my gallery shows.

After years of indifference, and often discouraged by what is called "the art community" (whatever that means), Carmen Morin-Miller of the Morin-Miller Gallery on West 57th Street in Manhattan, gave me a solo-show in 1986. She was the first to detect uniqueness in my drawings and to encourage me to pursue my path of creating what I came to call my *Dream Drawings*, or my *Dada Drawings from the Guts*.

Indeed, those *Automatic Drawings* emanate from my most inner dream world, a world that lies deep below the level of consciousness, which explains their unforeseen originality.

3. Becoming a Dada Painter

When I grew up, we had two pianos at home, but I wanted to play the violin. My father said: "When you know how to play the piano, I'll buy you a violin." After seven years of expensive piano lessons, they gave up on me and I never got my violin.

My father had a beautiful oil paint set, but wouldn't let me use it. "When you know how to draw and use

167

water colors, I will buy you an oil color set," he said. Of course, that never happened either.

Since parents make sure to never repeat their own parents' mistakes, I bought my son - Rudi Junior - his own oil color set for his 6th birthday, on October 27, 1976, to be exact. That night - at age 39 - I held my first oil color brush in my hand and showed my little son how to copy a landscape painting by Camille Corot. I finished it at four o'clock in the morning. That very night I became an avid painter and remained so ever since.

Actually, I became obsessed with painting my own interpretations of old master and Impressionist paintings. I painted from small images of different dimensions than the originals and finished them in the impressionist manner: all within a few hours or days.

After a while, I convinced myself that I was a great painter. Then, one day in 1984, an accomplished master told me "Oh yes, what you are doing is really nice craftsmanship, but you are missing the other sixty percent of what makes a good artist, which is to come up with your own creative subjects."

I didn't give up, and by 1986 I was able to paint with oil on canvas a whole series of my own impressionist-style magnifications of very small objects, including pine tree cones, a match box, my wife Angelika's left eye, and her knee.

By the fall of 1989, at my painter-friend Michael Irmer's studio in Dusseldorf, I managed for the first time to break through my rational thought process onto my subconscious level. I was awe struck, however, that my canvases had become almost entirely black. What followed was what I came to call my *dark period*, followed by the next stage of *Between Spirit and Matter*, which would become my ongoing style for an entire decade. During this time, my paintings gradually begun to lighten up, until they finally became vibrantly colorful, full of cadmium yellows and light reds.

I had become an abstract painter and sculptor with a logical sequence of an ongoing evolution, and used almost any painting material and randomly found objects, turning them into collages and sculpted pieces that were distinctly reminiscent of my own inner self.

Today, after many agonizing years of artistic and personal struggles, I am entirely comfortable to call myself an accomplished painter and sculptor.

In 2009, I did my first super large *Dada-Action Painting* at the spacious QCC Art Gallery/Museum in Queens, New York. It is an 80-foot by 83-inch canvas, which I painted in a mere ninety minutes and produced a film that can be seen on You Tube.

4. Sculptomania: Reverse Engineered

Often in life we do things without rationalizing or even questioning our motives, only to find out later that we did it subconsciously for a specific purpose that becomes rational only in hindsight. One such example is the case of my *Reverse Engineered Sculptures*.

Twenty-five years ago I begun to make sculptures of randomly found objects and of antique (two hundred years old) tools that I had brought along from Europe. I assembled them into sculpture pieces, which in 2001 I came to call "reverse engineered." Only recently, as I studied more closely the works of the Dadaist and Surrealist artists, did I realize the close relationship of my sculptures with the works of Marcel Duchamp's *Readymades*, which André Breton defined as "an ordinary object elevated to the dignity of a work of art by the mere choice of an artist." (Tout Fait.com:The Marcel Duchamp's On-Line Journal 02/25/05)

Well then, that's what I have been doing for the past quarter century, without even realizing that I was taking the idea of a readymade to a different level. By bringing several readymade pieces together, the initial object changed its appearance as a tool and became something more complex, which I came to name "Reverse Engineered Readymades."

One illustrative example of a Reverse Engineered Readymade is the *Bucking Horse*, a combination of an old stirrup with a leather strip, an old metal file, an ax and two very different antique pieces of wood drills: all used about two hundred years ago in a Swiss farm house. Each of the composing elements was a readymade tool that had served a specific purpose, but their combination made them become building blocks of an art piece that embodies a different idea, as it carries the distinct looks of a bucking horse.

5. My Path to Becoming a Dada Writer

Traditional Poetry

The word goes that good poetry does not rhyme. Recently, I even read that "Poems that don't rhyme are more meaningful."

I couldn't disagree more. Poems that don't rhyme are more often than not an easy way out for amateurs who don't know how to express their feelings at the much higher level of a formal poem that *does* rhyme. As far as I am concerned, way too many poems about emotions, love, nature etc. are justifying the common blame of being simplistic, plump and unsophisticated.

Yes, writing a rhyming poem that expresses precisely what you want to say, that is written in stringent line measures, and on top of all does perfectly rhyme, feels like playing a three-dimensional chess game and is quite stressful. But it is the ultimate poetic art form.

One problem when writing formal poetry in the above sense is that for a combination of perfect rhythms, melodies and rhymes, the poet needs filling words, which over time become a sort of second nature. In that sense, whenever I write stories in prose after composing poetry, I need to go over my text several times to eliminate filling words and make my writings look more streamlined and direct.

I have written hundreds of poems, first in German, and later in English. While, after many years of practice, writing poetry in my native German language now flows easily out of my pen; my naturally limited English vocabulary was a rather painful and tedious experience. This all the more as - after German and French - English is really my third language. Nonetheless, I persistently continued to write poetry in several languages, although I still nourish my (probably hopeless) optimism for English to become for me as easy as my native German, at least as far as the written word is concerned. As for my (incurable) accent, nobody can hear it when reading my poetry or prose.

For illustration purposes, I enclose two of my poems, a traditional one of a New York City subway event, and two recent ones from what I call my *Dada-Poms* collection:

Here is the traditional poem, written in 2000:

The Flying Smile

I rode a New York subway car,
And many hollow eyes
Surrounded me; they looked so far
Remote from hopes and lies.

Above that dungeon-like seclusion
And out of focus stare
There lay a cloud of disillusion
Quite heavy in the air.

Then, suddenly within that pile
Of cattle on the chase,
I caught a warm and friendly smile
straight from a lovely face.

It was so short, it was so fast,
It came from far away,
But even though it didn't last
Its beauty changed my day.

Dada-Poms

In good old Dada tradition, where the sound of words is more important than their content, I recently wrote a nonsensical "sonnet," written in my own Dada-Language. It is inspired by Johann Wolfgang von Goethe's famous poem *The Fisherman*:

The Story of Quig

There was a quampa in the gosh,
It had a bolo mang,
Yet while its baba was a mosh,
It never lala bang.

A quig came by and saw the gosh
"Polala manga tune?"
The quampa quizzled notabosh
"Ya mama cola pune!"

Su whereupon the quig begued
"Po quara nuna lee
Sopanagur quelesta gued
Ne bama never Bee!"

And, finally, there is my recent "Six-language Dada-Pom" written in Latin, Italian, German, English, French and Spanish:

In Vino Veritas
(6-Sprachen-Gedicht)

Nel mezzo del camin von meinem Leben
I drank the wine, qui est si bon, von meinen Reben;
ya no me souviens what time I went to bed,
pero ich weiss genau: the wine was red,
because das Weisse de mes yeux was rather rot
y en mi cama, from that wine, I felt halb tot.
Ein Glück nur que mon Dada kept me sane,
sinon le sense von dem Gedicht would be in vain.

Auf alle Fälle lautet die Conclusion:
De temps à autre Dada breeds confusion!

173

Writing Prose

It is one thing to write and then to have a pile of fading manuscripts laying around in the faint hope of handing them over to a family friend who knows someone in a publishing house.

My case is different. I have been writing for many years - day after day - about all that happened during my crazy life. I have brought my life onto paper in long hand writing, as expressed in my childhood tales, in my grown-up stories and in my philosophical essays, always putting it in context to confer an insight for future generations of what the world was like before it became digital.

The reward for me as a writer comes from personal satisfaction. So many long-forgotten events and emotions suddenly come back to life when I re-read and enjoy some of these deeply buried (and often forgotten) memories that come to life through my stories and poems.

The Dada-Tales – Automatic Writing

In *Les Champs Magnétiques* (The Magnetic Fields), Breton and Soupault, came up with the principle of what they called *Automatic Writing.* It is a process of writing text that does not come from the conscious thought process of the writer who is unaware of what will be written, but is rather created at the spur of the moment.

I must confess that I find it too silly (and easy) to write entirely nonsensical stories by just lining up words and sentences that make no sense. My Dada-Tales, as demonstrated hereafter, are only half - or sometimes even less - nonsensical, and always confer an illusion in a sort of literary "trompe-l'oeil" manner to convey some halfway intelligent information.

6. My Dada-Tales: Writing "From The Guts"

On August 4, 2008, I had the idea -out of the blue- to write a "tale from the guts" by filling an entire blank page in the exact same manner as I was doing my "Dada-Drawings," meaning with text automatically written, without ever thinking more than a few words ahead, and never lifting my pen. And, by doing so, I filled an entire page within minutes, in the case of my first Dada-Tale in just twelve minutes. By keeping a scrupulous time record, I attempted to assure a strict minimum involvement of the brain, so I would really "write from the guts" and not have a whole line of consistent rational thoughts interfere with my project.

*

I continued to write those Dada-Tales in three different languages and soon will have a collection big enough to fill a small book. Here below are two samples of these Dada-Tales:

Pedicure
(First Dada Writing)

Hand written by Rudy Ernst without interruption on

August 4, 2008, from 7:20 to 7:32 pm.

"...And as I write this in my mother's tongue, and the sky above me is wiggling the toe of my sweet and tender wife in the wind that carries the airplane and the automobiles upon the setting sun in Japanese culture, far away from the upcoming Olympic Games, a fly is sitting on my knee, just below where they cut the skin to make the graft to my arm 43 years ago, upon which I am writing here with a point five millimeter pen that covers this white page, slowly, line after line, just above the underlying art book that rests on my tummy, which is covered by my blue tee shirt, and below my bathing suit that is patiently waiting for the swimming pool to become empty of those elderly ladies who betray the tranquility of the blue water in the sun, which is by now almost ready to set, while the wind is picking up to the point that I have to hold my book and pen firmly in my hands, so they are not being carried away into the noise of yet another airplane above me, while the clouds in their sheep-like appearance definitely show all the signs that the wind is blowing from the south, while - to the contrary - it whirls around in circles here on the 44th floor of this Manhattan building, with Angelika's neatly pedicured red toe nails swinging slightly in the wind, and the sirens of a by-passing ambulance car down at the Lincoln Center reminding the untouched mind that all is not as well in the world as my 67 trillion cell strong cell colony that enjoys being still alive, even though it is not easy to hold the darn thing together ... just imagine!

176

Just imagine how cool it would be if all the living things in the Universe were singing the song of IMAGINE, and all the Quebec buses were not to crowd the entrance to the Strawberry Fields to the point that the yellow and the white flowers there are praying every night to the moon that the next day at sunrise the tourist nightmare would end and all the losers of the world would stay home. But wait, where would all the money come from if all the losers of the world would suddenly stay home? And would all the losers of the world stay in bed and produce new losers? Is that the explanation why we are soon going to be seven billion people on this planet?"

*

The result of my first "Dada-Tale" was so encouraging and well received by my friends in the literary field that I decided to keep going and write many more stories of that same nature. I got into problems with my "sweet and tender" wife of forty years, though, who pretended to notice certain ego-alteration problems in me. But she couldn't stop me from doing what I had to do, just as artists should never ever be stopped...

All the same, I somehow continued those Dada-Tale stories on a more or less continual basis. Here is another of my Dada-Tales:

All Those Happy Trees

Dada Tale written on Friday, October 24, 2008

In New York City -- Central Park West –

from 8:41 to 8:59 am

"While it is difficult on a day that is gearing up to become another Black Friday, like a repetition of 1929, I must force myself to think of the moon and the stars and the sun, and all the little birds that are ready to face the winter here in Central Park, where the theme of central is everything as central as the birds still singing and the rocks still waiting to become animated in ways never seen by any human beings that have only been around for about five million years, as compared to those rocks that have been inanimate for about one billion years or so (give and take a few million), but not at all like the economy, which is now in the trillions and therefore compares very favorably to those rocks in Central Park, where the birds and the squirrels are still meeting on a daily basis and drinking tea together (or is it beer, or even champagne?), which shows you how irrelevant - in the mind of those flowers that surround the rocks - the idea of a crashing economy really is, compared to the crispy, lovely sun that is now rising over the discoloring leaves of the trees just above them, and more than happy (I mean the trees) that this year they have not been attacked by those mean and nasty bugs that took a lot of them down those past few years, knowing full well (I mean the bugs) that even though they are hiding these days, they will still be around in about five hundred million years, of which I can say that if they were not years, but rather dollars, I would feel very good to have them in my pocket, although I would be at a real loss about figuring out how to invest this money on a Black Friday, which reminds me of a very black night with no moon and only some nightingale singing its beautiful melody about fifteen years back in southwest Virginia, when the world was not yet in turmoil, but the old rocks here in Central Park still quietly smiling at all the crazy follies of all the happy little animals all around them..."

*

Writing Dada-Tales is a fun game for social gatherings. Here is a third party sample of a Dada-Tale that we did recently in our family. It demonstrates how each of you readers can engage in the writings of these subconscious gut-stories yourselves.

Susan's Dada Tale

Written on the Island of St. John, USVI

on January 2, 2009, from 6:16 pm-6:26 pm

Winsome House

"My island is St. John. St. John is my island, and I couldn't imagine living anywhere else. Who am I you ask? I am a gecko, and I run around in the forest and through the hills. One day they decided to invade my kingdom and they built a monstrosity in its place. It took some time to get used to. First there were newcomers from Alabama and all they were belly flopping in the pool, then came the scholarly couples from places like Cambridge, Massachusetts and Litchfield, Connecticut and they pulled the binoculars to their eyes and observed all the fauna around the house and the birds and bees in the sky. Soon they found me entertaining and watched me do much of nothing. Ha! I fooled them; I actually have quite an adventurous day. Then flash forward to now, I'm not sure what to make of the group yet. A group of foursome, a language I recognize a little another completely foreign to me. They don't bother me much, the occasional "oh what a cutie" from the peculiar girl."

7. Film Making: Pulling It All Together

Film making is magic, and digital film technology came a long way since 1916, the beginning of the Dada movement.

Upon the passage into the new Millennium, it became evident that digital technologies and the Internet would become the dominant factor in the future. In 1997, I joined ArtNet and bought the book "Photoshop in 12 Easy Lessons." That was going to be easy: One single hour every day would turn me into an accomplished Photoshop scholar in just 12 days!

That was then. After two years of serious efforts, I finally became comfortable in the use of this fabulous tool and made a series of images, which came to be called as *CAA–Computer Aided Art*. I took a number of my painted canvases, digitized them, and then manipulated them in Photoshop.

Encouraged by the results, and as I had become "infected with the digital virus," I then ventured into the moving image. The study of *Final Cut Pro*, the state of the art program for professional film makers, took me another five years to get familiarized with, but the results paid off. With the help of today's fabulous (small) digital movie cameras, I became able to express my dreams, my writings, my musical compositions, my drawings, paintings and reverse engineered sculptures in that new film medium, which offers almost unlimited possibilities of expression.

Chapter 10

Activate Your Dada-Gene!

1. Now is the Time

More than twenty years back, I was involved in a real estate project that brought me close to some of Manhattan's poorest residents. During those days, I learned how many of these families were able to laugh and rejoice around a lavish family dinner table amidst the cruelest economic hardship. They didn't know where the money for the next meal was going to come from, yet were able to forget their troubles and royally enjoyed a moment of happiness.

*

The prospect of happiness is generated from our most inner self. While it is true that living on the edge of economic disaster breeds anxieties and is adverse to happy feelings, it is also correct that our primary source for happiness originates from the very core of our personality.

This is why today, times are right to activate your Dada-Gene!

*

I have demonstrated throughout this book how the initial Dadaists themselves often had a more positive approach towards life than the prevailing view generally suggests.

By introducing the notion of the Dada-Gene, I have chosen to take my positive approach to an even higher level and turn it into a positive idea altogether. By perceiving it as an uplifting gene that each one of us carries within, Dada thus becomes a precious instrument of rejuvenation and positive thinking in a world increasingly troubled by turmoil and negativities.

In the opening essay to his first novel, *Bibliothèque de mon oncle*, in 1832, the famous Swiss/French artist, writer and poet Rodolphe Toepffer (1799-1846) wrote under the title *The School of Leisure* how important it is to detach ourselves from time to time from the constraints of our daily lives and take refuge in the contemplation of minuscule natural objects, such as "Fixing the attention on a certain leaf," "Contemplating a spider web," or "Spit onto a certain cobblestone on our pathway..." - "What could a man be, or become," Toepffer asks, "who has never experienced this important stage in his life? He becomes like a steam engine, aimlessly thrusting from Liverpool to Manchester, without ever resting and taking time out..."

*

If Toepffer affirmed this to be the case at the beginning of the Industrial Revolution in the 1830s, how much more important would such a *School of Leisure* be in our present times.

183

2. We All Carry the Dada-Gene Within

Lao Tse said: "Without going out your door, you can know the ways of the world." This Lao Tse quote also applies to your Dada-Gene. Indeed, you have it all within your own body, which has gone through the entire evolutionary chain, from the minute you were conceived, all the way to the present stage of your adulthood.

Recently, while writing this book, a letter with a small slogan came into my hands. It read: "Discover the artist in you!" That's when it dawned on me that activating our Dada-Gene might partially be just that: the discovery of our own inner artist.

That Dada-Gene enables us to isolate ourselves from the nasty influence of the outside world and search for our own self in the midst of "Samsara," the Wheel of Suffering. It urges us into self-expression, artistic or not, and into the pursuit of happiness. As we open our senses to an alternative way of life by thinking out of the box, and as we begin to be our true selves, we rediscover so many small pleasures that were left on the wayside.

This approach is our search for happiness and inner protection against a world that is becoming increasingly unstable. A search for self-realization, which may end up either in artistic expressions, or simply in a state of pleasure for finding beauty and harmony, as we open our senses to the microcosm of nature.

Jean Arp wrote in his diary that his aim was "To destroy the rationalist swindle for man and incorporate him again humbly in nature." And while the Dadaists composed and read nonsensical poems and argued in nihilistic terms against the horrors of war, they actually upheld the basic laws of harmony in nature.

3. Boredom: The World's Greatest Plague

I never did drugs, but yes, I indulge in sharing a good bottle of wine with my wife for our daily meals. Wine is not a drug, as is generally believed, and it doesn't have to be expensive.

I firmly maintain that one doesn't have to do drugs to have fun in life. Twenty years ago, a friend told Angelika (my wife): "Who needs drugs if he is around Rudy!" I took that as a great compliment.

We have about 25,500 days to live, day by day, from the time we are born until we die, and every such second goes by and can never be recovered again. We can lose money and make it back, but we can never make back time.

And yet, our world is plagued with boredom, which is really the ultimate experience of losing time. To compensate, many of us escape into virtual realities of countless sorts, unaware of the personal waste of time it represents. Countless (mostly young) folks out there have earphones plugged into their head; they watch TV or read newspapers while eating lunch; sports- and other fans live entire lives within their large sub-cultures; the celebrity cult is escalating into unseen proportions. Already people are shopping in California's sperm banks for celebrity look-alike babies.

The celebrity cult has become the status symbol of our times and a mirage of excitement, like a sort of anti-boredom drug. The celebrity addicts of the world are - of course - unaware that actors, like TV celebrities, are just "talents" who read, memorize and repeat those prewritten lines that they are asked to repeat in front of a camera. Any closer acquaintance with those actors usually results in every bit as much boredom as talking to another person who isn't very inspiring.

The celebrity cult is just another expression of boredom in our permanent attempts to escape the realities of daily life. We exchange our own precious time that will never return for an illusion from which the wake-up call to reality becomes ever more painful.

Many of these pseudo-exciting, passive spectator activities are but futile attempts to escape inner boredom and find excitement elsewhere. They leave us unaware that, by spending our time with pointless consumerism, we are wasting our precious lives, while moving away from the basic laws of our inner time clock.

One of those areas to escape boredom is the world of noise, which has passed from the environment of loud mechanical machinery and trucks directly into the earplugs of a whole new generation.

Hans Arp saw it all coming: "Soon silence will have passed into legend. Man has turned his back on silence. Day after day he invents machines and devices that increase noise and distract humanity from the essence of life, contemplation, meditation -- Tooting, howling, screeching, booming, crashing, whistling, grinding and trilling bolster his ego. His anxiety subsides. His inhuman void spreads monstrously like a gray vegetation." (source MMVII Quotations Book)

No matter what, the minute we quit our computers and unplug our earphones, we all have our feet grounded on the soil and not in cyber space. We cannot escape the notion of our own earth-bound existence in nature and the essentials that all humans live by: water, oxygen, hydrocarbons, sex - and time.

*

There is yet another dimension: Our society and culture have become all about planning ahead, living the dream of a better (materialistic) future. But, while living by expectations, we are missing out on the present. Our capability, thanks to the Internet, to instantly access any information that mankind ever created or discovered, is a dangerous path that distracts us from the many wonderful details all around that could bring happiness, if only we were ready and willing (or meanwhile even capable) of focusing on our surrounding world and enjoying the present moment. Instead, the notion of money has become the focal point and yardstick of every aspect of modern society.

The state of the art world reflects these attempts to escape reality. The idea of harmony has the stigma of an "old hat" in an environment dominated by dissonances and escapes into drugs, all futile attempts to run away from boredom.

Disharmonies have become the norm in music, painting, theatre, TV, movies and poetry, where they are considered to be "trendy" and "progressive."

While money has become synonym with the idea of "quality of life," such a one-sided materialistic view could well be seen as another escape from the notion of time and from the basic realities of our lives.

With 662 Trillion dollars of worldwide financial derivatives, we may well be at the threshold of financial and political turmoil, the likes of it we haven't seen in generations.

This is fertile ground for activating our Dada-Gene.

4. Dada-Gene, Religion and Ethics

Psychologists believe that the reason for humans to believe in God, or gods, is to shift the responsibility of coping with life, and its compelling need to make daily decisions, onto a higher authority, and, while believing in such a Superior Force, to get relief from life's unbearable burdens and grieves.

Hans Richter writes in *Dada Art*:

"The realization that reason and anti-reason, sense and nonsense, design and chance, consciousness and unconsciousness, belong together as necessary parts of a whole –this was the central message of Dada."
(Richter, p. 64)

*

Does that sound like Taoism: The Ying and the Yang? Nirvana and Samsara? God and the Devil? And doesn't that open the door for our Dada-Gene to bring us closer to a peaceful life and a state of mind free from craving, anger and other afflictive states? These words express indeed the exact opposite of the anger that the original Dadaists were officially nourishing back in 1916.

Dada, as updated and redefined, is now at peace with the world, has compassion for all, and is free from obsessions and fixations.

The Dada-Gene, as herein defined, is promoting a Buddha-like attitude that leads on a path towards happiness.

This has nothing to do with religions, those organized indoctrinations for the profit of a small ruling class, which has come to be a tragedy for almost two thousand years, during which religious teaching came to be used as a weapon.

It is all right to be a Christian, a Jew, a Muslim, or to have any other religious belief. What is not o.k. in my opinion is to be fanatical about it, trying to convince the rest of the world that one's faith is the only true religion that will ensure paradise on the other side of death, always ready to take it to new extremes and fight for it with the sword, if necessary.

Even today, as we pay lip service to the principle of separation between State and Church, the reality is that a large minority is still out there to permanently lecture us about "religious truth" by mingling the notions of religion, ethics, morals, laws and politics all together.

These people do not realize how much damage they are inflicting onto their own cause.

Imagine how much brighter the prospects for lasting world peace would become, if the basic principle of "live and let live" were to be fully understood and applied! If the countless differences of beliefs and faith were suddenly to be tolerated by all of humanity!

5. Become an Independent Thinker!

One of the negative results of repetitive work and taking orders from others is the loss of our ability to think independently. The European school system, unlike the U.S. method, is not based on multiple-choice selections to find the right answer among three or four choices.

Real life is never white or black, but rather the result of a multitude of gray zones, of choices that rarely require a yes or no answer. This is why the future usually doesn't turn out to be as good as you hope for, nor as bad as you may have feared.

By becoming an independent thinker after your regular work hours, you enhance your ability to resolve many such personal gray issues.

*

Start thinking about your own body! Don't go that "ask your doctor!" routine. Your doctor has learned the better part of the approximate 20,000 diseases currently known to biomedicine. How in the world can he determine which one is your particular problem, unless you have developed a habit to observe your own body and what the variance from its normal functions are! And how long is your doctor's visit? Ten or fifteen minutes? Do you really expect him to tell you exactly what is wrong with you, based upon just a few answered questions and a couple of lab results? Think about it. The only way your doctor can help you is if you have an intimate knowledge of your own body, so you can tell him exactly how your infinitely complex cell colony reacts to a large number of contributing factors to your health problems.

Unlike a crossword puzzle, thinking is asking questions and seeing the answers in context, as opposed to compiling information in linear or alphabetical ways, like in dictionary listings.

As you follow the path of independent thinking, rather than "consume" information, you will discover a myriad of new answers to what you believed to be "facts," and they will lead you to a much-enhanced quality of life, based upon your own independent thought process.

6. Activate Your Dada-Gene!

On November 2nd, 2009, Charlie Rose interviewed the famous Nobel laureate James Watson who had discovered the DNA over fifty years ago. Rose asked: "Of the three, intelligence, memory and drive, which one do you find to be the most important in life?" Without a moment of hesitation, Watson replied, "Oh, there is no question. Of course it is the drive."

*

Don't be a passive consumer. Be active, become a producer!

And is it really so much fun to escape into a world of computer games, to have permanent beat or rap music busting your eardrums, or exchange shallow texting messages that take up a good part of your day without leaving a record to build on? Or are such superficial activities just other escapes from "a world that otherwise sucks?"

I believe that the experience of rediscovering yourself, and becoming aware of your feet actually touching the ground of planet earth, creates a lot of new openings to have fun and satisfaction.

How? You have it all in you. Activate it! Listen to your body and search for the harmonious cords therein. It is your defense mechanism that enables you to withdraw every now and then from the craze of the world around you and, in a Buddha-like manner, become self-focused on your inner self, as symbolized by your belly button that is the center of your own world.

*

I know, it is not easy and the adverse pressures out there are enormous. But now that you have a reference point and have become resourceful, your next step is an act of creation to project something of your inner self onto the outside world. By doing so, you suddenly realize that you have just created an external relationship with your inner self.

Activate that drive in you, which James Watson is talking about, that drive that got this amazing man with an IQ of only 120 his Nobel Prize! Create something, artistic or not! Express yourself in one way or another! It could be sky diving, fishing, flying a kite, writing a story, building a table, or painting a portrait. Or just going back to school, tackle a whole new field of interest, become an opera fan, etc. The possibilities are endless.

Just as the Dadaists and Surrealists have created a relationship between their art and the spectators thereof, try to form a relationship with the field of your choice out there and yourself! Get involved, get that drive going and activate your Dada-Gene! Suddenly, you will realize that your environment begins to look at you in different ways, that you make new friends, that you come up with new ideas, that you become an interesting person to share company with.

Google has opened an enormously vast new universe for all of us. It used to be that we had to travel for a whole day just to go to a library and find a single piece of information. Now, the entire world is at our fingertips, just a mouse click away. Anything has become possible, and we don't even have to pay for it.

7. Join the Dada-Gene Crowd!

Join the Dada-Gene Community! Connect with large groups of people who share the same interests as you have. See how many others have activated their Dada-Gene. Try *www.DadaGene.com*. The possibilities are endless and you will never be bored again!

And now, I encourage you to pick up a pen and a letter size piece of paper and activate your Dada-Gene by writing your first Dada-Tale. Take an alarm clock to time yourself and make sure you don't put down your pen until you have reached the bottom of the page.

Let yourself be surprised by the outcome and the revelation of your most inner thoughts. And be honest with yourself: Don't cheat by pausing between words, or by trying to preconceive what you are going to write.

Writing Dada-Tales, by the way, is also great fun for family and other gatherings. If you don't put down your name, nobody will know who wrote your story when you read them aloud at the end of the experience.

Writing Dada-Tales will probably be a great revelation for you! You may experience the same amazement as I did about the inner workings of what I come to call my "guts" and what the Dadaists called "mechanical writing." Many unexpected words and ideas came out of these writing experiments.

I know: the older we get, the more we tend to find excuses against new beginnings. But old age is not an excuse to becoming inactive. It is never too late to start a new endeavor. Take an example from that lady who graduated from university at age 92! Or the other one who became an opera singer at age 90 in her retirement home, because she didn't have the money to go through formal education when she was young.

8. A Few Final Words

1. One thing you may want to keep in mind: Don't take yourself too seriously. Always remember that if we could push all the atomic nuclei of our Planet Earth together, the entire globe would shrink to the size of a football!
2. And be an optimist! Hardship and disappointments are every bit a part of life, as the shadow is to light. Hope is the most important tool to overcome hardship, no matter how dim it may be. Indeed, by nourishing indestructible hope, you will find that, amazingly, and out of nowhere, a small light is beginning to shine on the horizon, and as you go on, it will magnify into a full-blown revelation of new opportunities that you never even dreamed of before.
3. Other than that: keep in mind that everything around us is Dada. Indeed.

*

APPENDICES

List of the Dada Artists

Here is a more complete list of the Dadaists. It also includes names that are generally figuring under different movements, but have created some Dadaist works.

Dada Visual Artists

Arp, Hans
Baader, Johannes
Baargeld, Johannes Theodor
Blumenfeld, Erwin
Crotti, Jean
Dreier, Katherine Sophie
Duchamp, Marcel
Eggeling, Viking
Ernst, Max
Freytag-Loringhoven, Baroness Elsa von
Golyscheff, Jefim
Grosz, George
Hausmann, Raoul
Heartfield, John
Höch, Hannah
Huelsenbeck, Richard
Janco, Marcel
Man Ray
Picabia, Francis
Prampolino, Enrico
Richter, Hans

Schad, Christian
Schamberg, Morton Livingston
Schwitters, Kurt
Stieglitz, Alfred
Taeuber-Arp, Sophie
Tschichold, Jan
van Doesburg, Theo
van Rees, Adya
van Rees, Otto
Wood, Beatrice

...And the Dada Writers Who Influenced Them

Aragon, Louis
Arensberg, Walter Conrad
Ball, Hugo
Breton, André
Cravan, Arthur (Fabian Avenarius Lloyd)
Einstein, Carl
Eluard, Paul
Evola, Julius
Friedlaender, Salomo (Mynona)
Hennings, Emmy
Herzfelde, Wieland
Iliazd (Ilia Zdanevich)
Josephson, Matthew
Jung, Franz
Loy, Mina
Mehring, Walter
Péret, Benjamin
Ribemont-Dessaignes, Georges
Serner, Walter
Soupault, Philippe
Spengemann, Christof
Tzara, Tristan (Samuel Rosenstock)
(http://arthistory.about.com/library/artists/bymovement/bldada_artists.htm)

Art Movements Since 1880

Just as a reference, and to raise awareness to the level of complexity that the art scholars have to deal with, the following table lists the various art movements that came to life since the 1880s:

Modernism: 1880 to 1945

Post Impressionism 1880 - 1900
Expressionism 1900 - 1920
Fauvism 1900 - 1920
Cubism 1907 - 1914
Dada 1916 - 1922
Bauhaus 1920s - 1940s
Harlem Renaissance 1920s - 1940s
Surrealism 1920s - 1940s
International Style 1920s - 1940s

Modern & Post Modern: 1945 to Present

Abstract Expressionism 1945 - 1960
Op Art 1960s
Pop Art 1960s
(http://www.arthistoryguide.com)

Selected Bibliography

Books on Dada

Barr, Alfred H.,Jr.   *What is Modern Painting? –* The
                          Museum of Modern Art,
                          New York, 1970

Coutts-Smith,
Kenneth.   *Dada.* Studio Vista Limited, Great
                          Britain, 1970

Lippard, Lucy R.   *Dadas on Art.* Prentice Hall, 1971.

Hapgood, Susan   *Neo-Dada – Redefining Art 1958-62.*
                          Catalogue published by the
                          American Foundation of Arts, 1994

Huelsenbeck,
Richard   *Memoirs of a Dada Drummer.* Viking
                          Press, New York, 1969.

Huelsenbeck,
Richard   *En Avant Dada: Eine Geschichte des
                          Dadaismus.* Paul Stegemann,
                          Hannover 1920.

Motherwell, Robert
(Editor)   *The Dada Painters and Poets.*
                          George Wittenborn, Inc, 1951.

Pritzker, Pamela   *Max Ernst.* Leon Amiel Publisher,
                          New York, 1975

Richter, Hans — *Dada Art and Anti-Art (1964),* trans. by David Britt. Thames and Hudson, London 1997

Rubin, William S. — *Dada, Surrealism, and their Heritage.* The Museum of Modern Art, New York, 1967

Tzara, Tristan — *The gas heat: the Dada anti-masterpiece of drama.* Translated by Eric v. d. Luft – Gegensatz Press, N. Syracuse, New York, 2008

Warlick, M. E. — *Max Ernst and Alchemy: a magician in search of myth.* University of Texas Press, 2001

General Books on Artists and Art Movements

Anfam, David — *Abstract Expressionism.* Thames and Hudson Ltd, London, 1990

Baltrock, Thomas — *Michael Irmer.* Wienand Verlag Köln, 1997

Baumann, Felix... — *Cézanne and the Dawn of Modern Art.* Hatje Cantz Verlag, Ostfildern, Germany, 2004

Burnham, Jack — *Beyond Modern Sculpture.* George Braziller Inc., New York 1968

Centre Georges
Pompidou

Jackson Pollock. 21 janvier - 19 avril 1982. Centre Georges Pompidou – Musée national d'art moderne. Paris, 1982

Chevalier, Denis

Paul Klee. Crown Publishers, New York, Bonfini Press Press, Naefels, Switzerland

Chipp, Herschel B.

*Theories of Modern Art.*University of California Press, Berkeley, Los Angeles and London, 1968

Deutscher
Taschenbuch
Verlag

Lyrik des expressionistischen Jahrzehnts. Munich, 1962

Dorra, Henri

Symbolist Art Theories, A Critical Anthology. University of California Press Ltd. London, England 1994

Editions Gemini

Gauguin – Les Peintures Immortelles. Kina Italia S.p.A., Milan

Fletcher, Valerie J.

Alberto Giacometti. Smithsonian Institution. Printed in Hong Kong by China Printing Company, 1989

Gilot , Françoise

Matisse and Picasso – Friendship in Art. Doubleday, New York, 1990

Harrison, Charles
& Charles Wood

Art in Theory 1900-1990 – Anthology of Changing Ideas. Blackwell Publishers Ltd, Oxford, UK, 1993

Hess, Walter

Dokumente zum Verständnis der modernen Malerei. Rowohlt Taschenbuch Verlag GmbH, Reinbeck bei Hamburg, 1956

Keller, Horst

Vincent van Gogh. Die Jahre der Vollendung. Verlag M. DuMont Schauberg. Köln, 1977

Kunsthaus Zürich

Picasso 11. September bis 30 Oktober. Berichthaus, Zürich 1932

Mailer, Norman

Portrait of Picasso as a Young Man. The Atlantic Monthly Press, New York, 1995

Mann, Carol

Modigliani. Thames and Hudson Ltd, London, 1980

Milner, Richard

Darwin's Universe – Evolution from A to Z. University of California Press. Ltd. London, England

Pritzker, Pamela

Ernst. (Max Ernst) – Leon Amiel, NewYork, 1975

QCC Art Gallery

An American Odyssey 1945/1980. Industrias raficas Afanias, 2004

Savas, Georgianna

eyes on stamos – a sister's memoir – a brother's wishes. Printed in Greece in 2005

Serna, Ramon
Gomez, de la   *Dalí.* The Wellfleet Press, Secaucus,
                      NJ 1988

Stevens, Mark &
Swan, Annalyn   *de Kooning – an American Master.*
                      Alfred A. Knopf, New York, 2005

Warhol, Andy   *Graphic Works.* QCC Art Gallery
                      Press, New York, 2006

General Literature

Baudrillard, Jean   *Simulations.* Semiotext and Jean
                      Baudrillard, 1983

Hochhut Rolf   *Die grossen Meister – Europäische
                      Erzähler des 20. Jahrhunderts.*
                      Bertelsmann Verlag, Gütersloh,
                      1962/6

Kafka, Franz.   *Sämtliche Erzählungen.* Fischer
                      Taschenbuch Verlag,
                      Frankfurt, 1970

Jung, C.G.   *Erinnerungen, Träume, Gedanken.*
                      Buchclub Ex Libris, Zürich, 1962

Eastern Philosophies

Lao Tsu.   *Tao Te King* -Translated by Victor H.
                      Mair. Bantam Books,
                      New York, 1990

Dalai Lama,
His Holiness,   The *Essential Teachings*. North
               Atlantic Books, Berkley, California,
               1994

Hesse, Hermann   *Siddhartha*. MJF Books, New York,
               © 1951by New Directions Publishing
               Corporation

Kaplean,
Roshi Philip   *Awakening to Zen*. Shambhala,
               Boston 2001

Rinpoche,
Akong Tulku   Taming the Tiger. Tibetan
               Teachings. Random house Ltd,
               U.K., 1995

Thich Nhat Hanh *no death, no fear – Comforting
               Wisdom for Life* – Riverhead
               Books, New York 2002

Thich Nhat Hanh *Being Peace.* Parallax Press,
               Berkeley, California.
               United Buddhist Church, Inc. 1987

Papers and Articles

Egbert, Donald D. The Idea of Avant-Garde in Art and
               Politics. Leonardo, Vol. 3, No.1
               (Jan. 1970) pp75-86, The MIT Press

Girst, Thomas   Rarities from 1917: The Blind Man
                     No.1, The Blind Man No.2 and
                     Rongwrong. Tout-fait Collections
                     Vol.1/Issue3 CASP/ASRL -
                     December 2000

Higgins, Dick   *INTERMEDIA.* LEONARDO, Vo. 34,
                     No. 1 pp. 49-54, 2001

Jessup, Bertram   *Truth as Material in Art.* The Journal
                     of Aesthetics and Art Criticism,
                     Vol. 4, No. 2 (Dec. 1945)
                     pp.110-114. Blackwell Publishing

Klein, Lee   *Art on the Eve of Destruction.*
                     Performing Arts Journal 75,
                     pp 20-25, 2003

Pogrebin, Robin   *Tight Times Loosen Creativity.* The
                     New York Times, Arts Section,
                     Wednesday, May 20, 2009

Saylor, Charles   *Mixing of Living Things and
                     Weapons in Roman Literature and
                     Dada Art.* Classical Mod Lit 25 no 1
                     Spr 2005. The H.W. Wilson
                     Company 1982-2005

Turvey, Malcolm   *Dada between Heaven and Hell:
                     Abstraction and Universal
                     Language in the Rhythm Films of
                     Hans Richter.* The MIT Press,
                     October, Vol. 105, Dada
                     Summer 2003, PP.13-36

White, Michael *Johannes Bader's Plasto-Dio-Dada-Drama: The Mysticism of the Mass Media.* Modern/*modernity* Vo. 8, No. 4, pp 583-602. John Hopkins University Press, 2001

A Personal Thank You

My wife Angelika is as much a saint as an angel for putting up with me for forty years of married life. In the context of this book, she was instrumental in getting me out of my loop with a myriad of loose ends. Her methodical legal mind showed me the way out of the maze.

Index of
Selected Artists

Printed in Great Britain
by Amazon

38198102R00117